OCKHAM

OCKHAM

STUDIES AND SELECTIONS

STEPHEN CHAK TORNAY

S. Th. D. (Vienna) M. A., Ph. D. (Chicago)
Instructor in Philosophy
University of Utah

The King's Library

LA SALLE   ILLINOIS

THE OPEN COURT PUBLISHING COMPANY

1938

PREFACE

WILLIAM OF OCKHAM stands out from a background of the medieval twilight as a peculiarly neglected figure. This regrettable neglect may be explained by the historical circumstances connected with Ockham's works. Of the works attributed to him we know of twenty philosophical and theological treatises, eight of which are in print and twelve in manuscript. He wrote eleven political treatises, five of which were printed and six are in manuscript. This means that only forty-two per cent of Ockham's works was ever printed. If we add that his printed works were never re-edited after the year 1675, the scarcity of books about him may be explained by the difficulty in consulting the original sources.

The neglect which William of Ockham has suffered is justly to be resented if we consider the fact that the Oxford Franciscan is generally accepted as a philosopher of first-class importance. His significance grows to almost epochal dimensions if we follow up the tremendous influence his nominalism or terminism exerted on posterity. It may be safely stated that the philosophical development of our modern period, empiricism and subjectivism, anti-intellectualism and pragmatism, and our positivistic preoccupations, can be traced to the cell of the restless and energetic Franciscan and to his nominalism. He is not only the *Inceptor omnium Nominalium monarcha,* the *Invictissimorum Nominalium inceptor,* the *Achademie Nominalium princeps* and the *Nominalium antesignanus*[1] but a very prominent herald of modern philosophy.

[1] Ancient titles of Ockham quoted in Überweg's *Grundriss der Geschichte der Philosophie* (Berlin, 1928), II, 575.

The importance of the place which Ockham occupies in the continuity of Western philosophical thought was brought out clearly by Windelband[2] and by several more recent writers. Indeed, his sun has been rising during the last few years with undeniable evidence. The *Venerabilis Inceptor*,[3] whose philosophical personality used to be more or less that of a distinguished stranger, is rapidly taking the place which he rightly deserves in the history of thought. His face has been placed in sharp relief by Erich Hochstetter's monograph on Ockham's metaphysics and epistemology (Berlin, 1927), by Simon Moser's presentation of his natural philosophy (Innsbruck, 1932), and by Ernest A. Moody's outstanding essay on his Logic (New York, 1935), to mention only the very latest works. However, the great classic on William of Ockham, the book which will give an all-comprehensive survey of his whole philosophy and will point out his significance in the development of philosophical movements in a monumental manner, is still in the womb of time.

The present volume makes no claim for greatness. It intends to give a brief presentation of the whole of Ockham's philosophy in the form of short essays and original translations illustrating the various fields of his interest. The purpose of the book is to offer both to the college student and to the advanced scholar important source material for a deeper understanding of the lines of thought which through a continuous stream resulted in the intellectual orientation of the present. Without a first-hand knowledge of the medieval inheritance, Francis Bacon and Descartes will always

[2] Windelband, *A History of Philosophy* (New York, MacMillan, 1923). *See* Index on Nominalism and Terminism.

[3] Ockham was only an "inceptor" in theology and never received his B.D. degree.

impress us as types of a *"deus ex machina."* The
helpless and uncertain groping of a modern free lance
in philosophy, who likes to start everything anew, is
undoubtedly due to a lack of acquaintance with the
"dark interval" which separates for many the outgoing
light of Hellas and the rising day of the moderns.
Students of philosophy burdened with this concealed
"heel of Achilles" will always feel unsafe and vulner-
able because they are incapable of seeing problems in
perspective. Fortunately, the genetic significance of
the study of medieval thought is probably appreciated
now more than at any other time during the last few
hundred years, and the author who presents medieval
material has no longer to offer apologies.

The specific significance of Ockham's philosophy,
known as the nominalistic line of thought, is to be
sought in the fact that it opens up the source to which
some of the most essential modern philosophical problems can be traced. The simple Franciscan, threading
the weary way of a defiant warrior in the outgoing
Middle Ages was unaware of the import of his achieve-
ments. In the background of the centuries, however,
he stands out today as one of those rare figures who
marks out the crossroads. The fruitfulness of studying
his thought should establish the legitimacy of these
eulogies.

The first part of this book is a series of essays explan-
atory to the selections from the works of Ockham which
constitute the second part. Two of the essays, the one
on Ockham's Nominalism, the other on his Political
Philosophy, are versions of articles which appeared in
the *Philosophical Review* (May, 1936) and in *Church
History* (Sept. 1935). The selections present the essence of Ockham's philosophy topically arranged. Some

of the material selected introduces uninterrupted por-
tions, other parts give a symposium of representative
passages characterizing various fields arranged in such
a manner as to give the effect of coherent reading material. It is expected that the advantages to be gained
for the busy scholar by thus getting the essence in a
nutshell will offset in some measure the inadequacies
of fragmentary presentation.

Two names have to be remembered with the utmost
gratitude in connection with the progress of this investigation. First, Professor Charles W. Morris, whose
constant encouragement and assistance was the chief
factor which made the appearance of this book possible. I am indebted to him for his kindness in lending
me his film of Ockham's *Logic*. The other name is
that of Professor Thomas V. Smith, whose command
of the English language came many a time to my help
in rendering the text in its present form. I have also
much for which to thank Dean Richard McKeon and
Dr. Ernest A. Moody without whose suggestions some
of the more difficult sentences would have remained
unsolved. Grateful acknowledgements are due to Professor B. Roland Lewis, Professor Louis C. Zucker,
Miss Elizabeth Cary, and Mr. Waldemer P. Read for
their valuable critical marks, and to Miss Henrietta
Henderson for her help in reading the proofs.

                              STEPHEN CHAK TORNAY.
The University of Utah,
December 1937.

CONTENTS

PART ONE

STUDIES

OCKHAM'S NOMINALISM

THE FOLLOWING is an attempt to delineate Ockham's essential contribution, his nominalistic approach to the solution of logical, epistemological, and metaphysical problems, an achievement to which he owes his chief fame.

The story of philosophical development in the West centers, undoubtedly, in the problem of the nature of conceptual thought. The universal or class concept, discovered by Socrates as the rock of knowledge, extended by Plato to metaphysical dimensions, and developed by Aristotle as the indwelling principle of all actuality, was eagerly accepted by both the Augustinian and Thomistic lines of thought as the surety to guarantee the solidity of science and life. Logic was projected into ontology as a pertinacious pursuit of self-assertion to impose a human perspective upon the world.[1] The stubborn facts of human defeats were bound to open the eyes sooner or later to the futility of such anthropocentrism. Realism, which had been dominant throughout the centuries of the Middle Ages, received its first serious blow under the onslaughts of Roscelin and Abelard in the middle of the twelfth century. The historical rôle, however, of undermining its foundations in a fatal manner, was reserved to William of Ockham. After him moderate realism found its home for the most part in the seclusion of institutions dedicated to the cultivation of medievalism.

[1] Reference is made in this connection to Bergson's criticism of the philosophy of Form, in his *Creative Evolution*, Chapter IV, pp. 304-329.

The road to his task was immediately prepared by what was called in Ockham's time the *Logica moderno-rum,* a logic presenting a reborn Phoenix-bird of long forgotten grammatical interests once cultivated by the Stoics, and later by Donatus (c. 350) and Priscian (c. 500). This logic as developed at the end of the thirteenth century was a grammaticized logic and a logicized grammar.[2] It dealt with the nexus between grammatical forms and thought-forms. The chief representative of this new logic was the *Summulae logicales* of Petrus Hispanus, a book that had a dominating influence up to the sixteenth century. In the famous seventh chapter of the *Summulae,* Petrus Hispanus develops the *proprietates terminorum,* a treatise dealing with the grammatico-logical properties of words, such as: *significatio, suppositio, ampliatio, appellatio, restrictio, distributio, exponibilia.* The chief property of a word is considered the signification with the supposition following it. "The signification," says Petrus Hispanus, "is prior to supposition; they differ in that the signification belongs to a word, while the supposition belongs to a term already composed from the word and signification."[3] The new logic undertook to investigate the various modes of signification and initiated a new literary form called *de modis significandi* widely cultivated in the ensuing period.

There can not be the least doubt that the widespread cultivation of grammaticized logic with its unceasing investigation of the significatory modes of the noun, pronoun, verb, adverb, participle, conjunction, preposition, and interjection, was the immediate occasion for

[2] Carl Prantl, *Geschichte der Logik im Abendlande,* (Leipzig, 1867) Vol. III, Chap. 17, p. 73.

[3] Petrus Hispanus, *Summulae logicales,* VII, 1, 1, 2 (f. 209 A) in Prantl, op. cit., chap. 17, p. 51, Anm. 201.

Ockhamist nominalism. Logic, which used to have the character of a scientific methodology, now, by its intimate connection with grammar, became a *scientia sermocinalis,* that is, a science dealing not with aspects of truth and error, but with meanings and significations. Grabman translates the word *grammatica speculativa* as *Bedeutungslehre,* and Heidegger the doctrine of the *modi significandi* as the doctrine of *Bedeutungsformen.*[4] Logic, which used to teach *vere loqui,* began after its alliance with grammar to teach *recte loqui.* Interest was centered now not on the right relationship to the ontological realm in order to obtain truth, but on the content of thought immanent in words, and on the function of the various forms of thought. Thus, the *modi essendi et subsistendi* fell more and more into oblivion and the *modi significandi et intelligendi* became the center of interest. Stress was laid on the "intentional inexistence"* rather than on their ontological referents. With forerunners, such as Durandus of St. Pourçain (c. 1270-1334)[5] and Peter Aureoli (d. 1322)[6] it was William of Ockham who came to unfold more fully the implications of this changed interest and to develop on its basis his nominalistic theory of knowledge.

[4] Martin Grabman, *Mittelalterliches Geistesleben,* p. 117.

*Franz Brentano, *Psychologie,* I, p. 115. "Every psychic phenomenon is characterized by what was called in the language of the Schoolmen of the Middle Ages an intentional inexistence of the object and what we may call a reference to a content, a direction toward an object or an immanent objectivity."

[5] *Sent.* II, dist. 3, q. 7, fol. 107, 1 Q, in Maréchal, *Le Point de Départ de la Métaphysique,* Bruges-Paris, 1923; "The universal does not precede the act of intellect, but rather is produced by the act of intellect."

[6] *Sent.* I, d. 23, a. 2, in Überweg, *Grundriss,* II, p. 527: "It is manifest that the aspect of man and animal in so far as it is distinguished from Socrates is a fabrication of the intellect and is nothing but a concept."

Ockham's epistemology centers entirely in the notions of signification and supposition. The task of epistemology is to investigate the problem of the possibility of knowledge. What is Ockham's position concerning this problem? How does he build the bridge which is supposed to connect the external world with the mind? His first task is to clear the ground by rejecting the "copy" or "species" theory. The realists in order to explain how the material world can affect the immaterial soul inserted, as intermediary between the two, the sensible and the intelligible species considered as something immaterial. The species was the vehicle whereby the copy or similitude of some extramental reality arises in us. Ockham rejects the sensible species as superfluous, and the intelligible species as impossible. For if matter cannot affect the immaterial soul, how can it produce the immaterial species? Again, if matter cannot act at a distance on the soul without the species, how can it produce the species at a distance?[7]

Having eliminated the "species" or intentional copies of things from the mind, Ockham had to square accounts with the theory which assumed a cognitive "adequation" between the intellect and the extramental thing. According to Aristotelian, or moderate, realism the universal concept or intention in which the species crystallizes itself by the efficiency of the active intellect has an ontological counterpart corresponding to it, conceived by Aristotle as immanent (ἐνυπάρχον) in the particular things. Truth is an adequation of the knowing mind with this ontological counterpart. To

[7] *Sent.* II, qu. 15, O. I am using the 1495 edition printed in Lyons, now the property of the library of the Peabody Institute, Baltimore, Md.

be sure, the *"universale in re"* is not a subsisting something in the thing. The form, as a universal, does not exist except in the mind.[8] Nevertheless, it is in the thing as the formal principle individualized in and by the material substratum. Says Saint Thomas: "For if we consider the nature of gender and species itself, as it is in singular objects (*prout est in singularibus*), we will find it somehow as the formal principle with respect to singular objects."[9] This formal element is the ontological foundation of our conceptual knowledge and the chief object of all scientific investigation.

This realistic account of the possibility of knowledge receives the most careful consideration from Ockham. His commentary to the *Sentences* of Peter Lombard contains a veritable arsenal of proofs against it.

From the immense number of arguments which Ockham lines up against the realistic universal we can present only a few typical ones.

Against the view of St. Thomas he argues thus: If the universal exists as something really distinct from the individual it must be numerically one and, therefore, something singular and not universal. But how could a singular thing as such exist in many things at once?[10] If humanity were a thing different from the singular individuals, one and the same thing would be in many individuals, which would be condemned in Judas and saved in Christ and, hence, there would be something condemned and miserable in Christ, which is absurd. In much the same manner, God could not,

[8] St. Thomas Aquinas, *Contra gent.* I, c. 65: "Universalia non sunt res subsistentes, sed habent esse solum in singularibus." *Contra gent.* I, c. 44: "Forma per modum universalem non invenitur, nisi in intellectu."

[9] *Summa theol.* I, qu. 85, art. 3.

[10] *Sent.* I, dist. 2, qu. 4, D.

then, annihilate an individual without destroying all the individuals of the same genus.[11]

Against the formal distinction of Duns Scotus this is his argument: It is impossible to distinguish the common nature from the individual difference formally without falling back to a real distinction. If "there is in Socrates a human nature which is contracted to Socrates by an individual differentia, which is not distinguished really, but formally, from that nature, we should have a thing which was universal and particular at the same time." Therefore "it is impossible to admit that in created things something differs formally without being distinguished really. But granting this distinction, the view is still untrue. If nature were common in that manner, it follows that there would be just as many species and genera as there are individuals."[12] In that case, consequently, there is no place left for a common nature. The objection that the universal is *of* the essence of Socrates and not the total essence of Socrates, does not have any strength. In that case "every individual would be an aggregate of an endless number of actual things, namely of those common features which are predicated of it."[13] This argument is directed specifically against the "*formalitates*" of Duns Scotus which were supposed to subsist actually in the particular.[14]

Against the third view maintained by such men as Aegidius Romanus (1247-1316) and Walter Burleigh (d. after 1343), which identifies the universal with

[11] *Summa tot. log.* II, 2, f. 25 v. B, in Prantl's *Geschichte der Logik,* Chap. 19, p. 350, Anm. 794.

[12] *Sent.* II, qu. 9, C. C.

[13] *Sent.* I, dist. 2, qu. 4, D.

[14] *Sent.* I, dist. 2, qu. 6: "Ista opinio est, ut credo, opinio subtilis doctoris, qui alios in subtilitate iudicii excellebat."

the particular, and yet nevertheless finds a ground to distinguish them by a quasi-mental distinction, Ockham points out that there is no justification whatever for such distinction. The intellect must not change the thing. If it is individual and particular, it should not be declared universal.[15]

The results of his attacks agains the realistic universal Ockham sums up in the following manner: there is no such a thing as a universal, intrinsically present in the things to which it is common.

After having discarded the realistic universal Ockham continues to work out in his own way the explanation of how knowledge is possible. It is precisely at this point that the *Parva Logicalia,* the seventh chapter of Petrus Hispanus' *Logic,* came to his help. By utilizing the new notions of speculative grammar he worked out a new theory of knowledge and arrived at his nominalism. For the discarded theory of *copy* and *adequation,* he substituted a new one: that of *sign* and *signification.* Between the two theories there is a world of difference. In Ockham's view all our conceptions are mental signs which signify the external things. "A sign is anything that, as apprehended, presents something else to cognition."[16] "The intention wherewith I understand men is a natural sign signifying man, just as natural as a sigh is the sign of infirmity or pain. It is a sign which can stand for men in mental propositions."[17] Signs, in so far as they stand in a proposition, are called terms, *termini.* "A term is nothing else but the subject or predicate of a proposition as signifying something.[18] The term is threefold:

15 *Sent.* I, dist. 2, qu. 7, L.   .
16 *Summa totius logicae,* I, 1, cap. 1.
17 Ibid., I, 15, f. 6, v. B.
18 Ibid., C. 2, f. 2, v. A.

written, spoken, and conceived. The words are signs subordinated to the concepts or intentions of the soul. First, the concept signifies something naturally and then, second, the word signifies that same thing. The concept or passion of the soul signifies whatever it signifies naturally; the spoken or written term, on the other hand, does not signify anything except by voluntary agreement. The spoken or written term can change its signification at discretion; the concept-term, on the other hand, never changes its signification at any one's pleasure."[19]   The important word in these preliminary remarks of Ockham is the word "natural." It gives us the clue to everything he has to say concerning the conditions and validity of knowledge. The bridge that he intends to build from the mind to the world will be constructed out of the steel of natural signification.

Our analysis of Ockham's gigantic efforts to build a bridge will fall into two parts, treating of the hither and thither sides of the structure devised to span the chasm between the mind and the world. Let us concentrate, first, on our side of the mind-world relationship and investigate *the nature of mental signs* in their *psychological aspect*. What is a mental sign considered in itself, in its entity as a mental fact? Ockham calls it an "intention of the soul" a word derived originally from Avicenna. "An entity in the soul meant to signify something is called the intention of the soul. This subsisting something in the soul which is a sign of the thing, and out of which mental propositions are composed, is sometimes called the intention of the soul, sometimes the concept of the soul, sometimes the pas-

[19] *Expos. aurea*, Perierm., Proem., in Prantl, op. cit.

sion of the soul, sometimes a likeness of the thing."[20]

Now, "what is that in the soul," we hear the author asking himself, "which is such a sign?" Ockham takes three views into account. According to the one, the mental entity that functions as a sign is a mere fictitious likeness, *quoddam fictum,* of the object without any psychological actuality of its own. It is a mere thought-out something, a purely logical fiction which is supposed to represent the external objects. Ockham eliminates this view on the same grounds on which he had cancelled the realistic "species." Both the psychological entity of the species and the logical entity of the *fictum* impede cognition and are superfluous. According to another opinion, the mental intention which signifies is some quality of the soul, distinct really from the act of intellect because it results from it, which as a resemblance of the external thing represents that thing. Even this view is against his famous law of parsimony, according to which "we should never employ a plurality of entities without necessity,"[21] or, expressed in another way "it is needless to recur to many entities when we can get along with fewer ones."[22] Therefore, he adopts the simplest view, which we also find with Durandus, according to which "the passion of the soul is the act of intellect itself. This seems to me," says Ockham, "the most probable of all opinions."[23]

This knowledge that the intention of the soul in its psychological entity is an act of intellect is to be extended now to the extremely important subclasses of

[20] *Expos. aurea,* Perierm., Proem., in Prantl, op. cit.

[21] *Sent.* I, d. 27, qu. 2, K. "Nunquam ponenda est pluralitas sine necessitate."

[22] *Summa tot. log.* I, 12, ed. Ven. 1522, fol. 6, r. A. "Frustra fit per plura quod potest fieri per pauciora."

[23] *Expos. aur.,* Perierm., Proem., in Prantl, op. cit.

the first and second intention. The first intention is any mental act which directly and immediately signifies one individual object, like Socrates, or a class of individual objects, like man, animal. The second intention, on the other hand, is a mental act signifying a first intention, expressing for instance some characters of it, such as genus, species, individuum, and so on. The first intention is called by Ockham a thing, that is, something psychologically subsisting in the soul, while the second intention is not a psychological but a logical fact with its essential quality of predicability. The first intention, as such, is a sign and stands directly for external things without involving any notion of predicability, while the second intention is always a certain mode of logical predication.

In connection with the division of intentions we should become acquainted with Ockham's division of "names" (*nomina*). "Names" which directly signify our intentions, be they of the first or second type, are called names of first imposition. Names which signify such names of first imposition—for instance noun, verb, substantive, adjective, adverb, are called names of second imposition. The word "father" applied to the meaning "father" is imposition in the first instance. The application of the word "noun" to the word "father" is imposition in the second instance.

The notion of second intention, being identical with that of the universal, leads us to the most important part of Ockham's epistemology. The universal in his opinion is an intention of the soul, which as a mental fact is something singular in the mind. "Every universal is one singular thing and is universal only by signification of many things. The universal is one and is a single intention of the soul meant to be predicated of many things; in so far, however, as it is a single form subsisting really in the intellect, it is called singular."[24] How now does the universal character enter into a singular intention? It enters by way of abstracting from various individual objects one and the same element, on the basis of which all of them can be held together in one representative act. This process is entirely natural and spontaneous without any planned activity of the intellect and will, and is to be understood in terms of a cause and effect relationship. The universals and second intentions simply appear in the mind as mental products caused spontaneously by the particular objects as heat is caused by fire, to use the very words of Ockham.[25] The origin of the universal, then, is traced to external objects, or rather, to the effects of those objects in the soul which are the intuitions.

Now in Ockham's doctrine every intention of the soul, whether first or second, intuited or abstracted, is significatory. Hochstetter, analyzing this significatory character of intuitions calls our attention to its remarkable resemblance to Helmholtz's theory of *Sinnliche Zeichen,* according to which "the same object exerting its influence under the same circumstances brings forth the same sign, and different impressions correspond always to different signs."[26] This preliminary intuition is the intermediary between the external object and the intellect, which leaves a certain trace in us exactly as in the modern doctrine of the substitute stimulus. This substitute stimulus may revive the original

[24] *Summa tot. log.* I, 1, c. 14.

[25] *Sent.* II, qu. 25, 0.

[26] Herman von Helmholtz, *Die Tatsachen in der Wahrnehmung,* S. 222 in Erich Hochstetter, *Studien zur Metaphysik und Erkenntnislehre Wilhelms von Ockham,* (Berlin, 1927) p. 118.

intuition and act in its stead as a cause with reference
to the intellect. Repeated causal actions of the external object or of the substitute stimuli create in us in
Ockham's expression "a certain habit,"[27] with an inclination to revisualize the previously sensed object.

The process of abstraction in these words is described entirely in terms of similar experiences caused
by objects, through intuitions or habits resulting in a
new or second intention: the universal. The distinctive mark of every universal is to be a sign for all the
individuals involved in the abstraction. "The intention
of the soul is universal, because it is a sign which can
be predicated of many."[28] The process of abstraction,
then, ends in an intentional sign, which reciprocally
refers back to the *inferiora* in a significatory manner
and is predicable of them.

In the notion of predicability we have reached the
very essence of the universal. Ockham is very emphatic in pointing out that, although the universal is
embedded in a psychological act, yet according to its
inmost essence it is not a psychological, but a logical
entity. He refuses to call the universal an idea, because ideas and images are psychological entities. To
quote the Venerabilis Inceptor: "The universal is not
some real thing having a psychological being (*esse subjectivum*) in the soul or outside of the soul. It has only
a logical being (*esse objectivum*) in the soul and is a
kind of fiction having the same sort of entity in the
logical realm as the external thing has in the psychological realm. Figments have no psychological being
in the soul, for then they would be real things, and a

[27] *Sent.* II. qu. 15, C and qu. 17, S. "Habitus quidam in-
clinans ad phantasiandum objectum prius sensatum."

[28] *Summa tot. log.* I, 1, c. 14.

chimera and centaur and other such things would all be
real things. There are, then, certain entities which have
only logical being. In the same way, propositions, syllogisms, and such other things as logic treats, have no
psychological being, but only a logical being: and so
their being is their being understood."[29]

To be sure, when Ockham calls the universals fictions, he is far from subscribing to the theory of *fictum*
or *idolum* which he refuted before. That theory was
an explanation of the psychological existence which
the first and second intentions have in the soul, while
this conception adds the logical character to second intentions or the universals, the psychological status of
which he described as acts of intellect.

The foregoing analysis of the abstraction was intended to point out the genesis of the universal in Ockham's epistemology and to bring to consciousness the
revolutionary shift which was performed by his trans-
planting the universal from the realm of ontology to that
of psychology and logic. When he put down the following simple sentence: "The second act (following
that of the intuition) *produces* the universals and the
second intentions and *does not presuppose them,*"[30] he
was writing a new chapter in the annals of history.
Again, when he unhesitatingly announced that if our
intuitions and abstractions, sensations and concepts are
mental signs, "we know only propositions, and any science, real or rational, deals exclusively with propositions as such,"[31] he initiated a new period in the history
of philosophy.

[29] *Sent.* I, dist. 2, qu. 8, F. "Ita quod eorum esse est eorum
cognosci."

[30] *Sent.* II, qu. 25, 0. "Et ille actus secundus producit
universalia et intentiones secundas et non presupponit eas."

[31] *Sent.* I, dist. 2, qu. 4, M.

So far we have been dealing with our side of the mind-world relationship in itself and in its psychological aspects. The second part of this essay will concentrate on the other side of this relationship, that is, it will deal with the possibilities of connecting the world with the mind. In other words, it remains to be seen, how the validity of knowledge can be established on the basis of Ockham's nominalistic epistemology.

Ockham accepts as a basic fact that the substratum of all knowledge is furnished to us from an extramental world by means of natural causation. Our sensations and intuitions are effects produced in our sensitive faculty by singular objects in the external world which act as causes. We are, to use his word, "moved" by externally originated sensory influences, whereby we begin to know the objects of the world.[32] Science, however, does not deal with concrete data exclusively. In Ockham's words: "Since all our knowledge derives from the senses, every science, too, originates from individual objects, although no doctrine should treat of singular things. Properly speaking, there is no science of individuals but of universals standing for individuals."[33] It is the realm of universals, then, which has to be examined carefully as to whether it is a public receiving station recording actual messages coming from the extramental world, or a mere private laboratory manipulating subjective elements in isolation.

Having eliminated the universal from the ontological world, Ockham had to face the task of saving the valid and objective character of conceptual knowledge. He

[32] *Sent.* I, dist. 2, qu. 7, F.
[33] *Expos. aur.,* Praedicab., De specie, in Prantl, op. cit.

had cut the ropes which were connecting the boat of
the mind to solid ground. Now he had to prove that
the signals which he installed were safe enough means
of maintaining contact with the shore. Ockham was
quite confident that he could find his orientation with
mental signs and their signification just as well as the
realists did with their own theory of copy and adequation.

The dangerous character of his doctrine of universals lies in the fact that Ockham explicitly compares
them with mental fictions, (*fictum, figmentum*). The
universal as such has no psychological being in his
theory. It is supported by the vehicle of an act of intellect, yet, as such, as universal, it is only a logical
entity in the soul and its being is its being understood.
Such a purely logical product has an unmistakable
similarity with mere mental inventions.

Nothing would be more regrettable for Ockham
than to see his theory sinking in the morass of sub-
jectivity. He insists that the universal is not a figment
like a chimera or something of that sort, but is a likeness (*exemplar*) related without any difference to the
external single things for which it stands.

The two apparently realistic expressions which occur
here: *exemplar* and *similitudo,* may be taken for the
fact that Ockham was willing to adopt the very words
of his adversaries rather than to give up the objective
validity of his universals. On closer investigation,
however, it is evident that his meaning is very different
from that of the realistic similitude between the *species
sensibilis* or *intelligibilis* and the external object. According to his opinion, knowledge based on the similarity of the object and its representation is impossible.
To quote him: "Nothing can be represented unless

the thing to be represented is known previously."[34]
Knowledge based on similarity would postulate *a priori*
elements in the mind. The following brings this out
very clearly: "When the knowledge of a similarity
produces the knowledge of that to which it bears a resemblance, to know the fact of similarity is not a sufficient cause for the intellect, but it is necessary to have
a habitual knowledge of that to which it bears a resemblance. Therefore, if somebody saw the statue of
Hercules, without knowing anything about Hercules,
he would not by that think rather of Hercules than of
Achilles, unless he knew Hercules first and there remained in him the habitual knowledge of Hercules."[35]
This realization of the impossibility of an *a priori*
knowledge brings him to the conclusion that knowledge
based on a similarity between object and representation
is altogether impossible.

What is, then, that similitude in the logical realm, on
the basis of which the universal can stand for external
things and can be predicated of them? It cannot be
the external similitude of the accidents of things
as we find it in the doctrine of Abelard and the
moderate realists in general. We do not know anything directly about those accidents. The representations we have from them do not show their characters
adequately. Ockham even goes so far as to say that
"the thing is not more present to the mind by the act
of intellect than Caesar is present to somebody by picture."[36] True to his Augustinian preoccupations he

[34] *Sent.* II, qu. 15, T: "Nihil potest per aliud representari
nisi representatum fuerit prius notum."
[35] *Sent.*, Prol. qu. 9, L.
[36] *Sent.* I, dist. 27, qu. 3, X: "Res non plus capit esse per
hoc quod intelligitur quam Cesar per hoc quod pingitur, nec
plus est presens intellectui per intellectionem proprie loquendo
et de virtute sermonis quam Cesar est presens alicui per pic-
turam."

states that the purely intelligible facts such as acts of
intellect, acts of will, pleasure, sorrow and the like,
which one can experience as internal, are known to us
with greater certainty than the things which fall under
the senses.

In what, then, lies this important notion of similarity? After what we know about his views on the superiority of inner experiences, we will find it quite
consistent when he says that it lies *in the similarity of
experience*. Repeated impressions of stones, for instance, produce in us a reiteration of the original experience when we touched stone for the first time. Because of the similarity of these impressions and on the
basis of such repeated and resembling experiences the
intellect molds them into an *exemplar*, a logical *fictum*,
into a meaning, quite in the sense of the *Bedeutungen*
of Husserl,[37] and this logical focus of accumulated
similar experiences is the universal which functions for
all stones, [38] signifies them, and stands or supposits for
them in logical propositions. The similarity, then, upon
which he founds his universal concept is a functional
similarity of resembling cognitive processes or experiences.

The road to this notion of the universal was prepared
for Ockham in Aristotle's account of how universals
originate. "Out of sense-perception," says the Philosopher, "comes to be what we call memory, and out of
frequently repeated memories of the same thing develops experience; for a number of memories constitute a single experience. From experience again originate the skill of the craftsman and the knowledge of
the man of science."[39] Ockham literally includes these

37 Überweg, *Grundriss*, II, p. 577.
38 *Quodlib.* I, qu. 14, in Prantl, op. cit.
39 *Analytica Posteriora*, II. 19, 100 a, 3-8.

words of the *Posterior Analytics* in his *Expositio aurea*
by saying: "Every science starts from individuals.
From sensation, which gives only singular things, arises
memory, from memory experimentation, and through
experimentation we get a universal which is the basis
of art and science."[40] These quotations give new clues
to the often repeated statement that Artistotelian empiricism is an introduction to nominalism.

How now does the logical meaning of accumulated
experiences connect with the external world? This is
explained by the following words of Ockham: "I understand by experience because I see the image of the
stone. The certainty of understanding the stone, however, comes by reasoning *from effect to cause*."[41] The
repeated similar experiences, recorded in the logical
realm, came as effects from the world by way of natural causation. Consequently, the universals which are
in the focal point of these effects are veritable Morse
signs conveyed by the electric current of natural causation. Ockham's logical realm operates very much like
an electromagnetic telegraph apparatus, where the signals caused by the electric circuit connect us with the
encircling world. There is probably no other conception to which Ockham would cling more tenaciously
than that of *natural signification*. "It is sufficient," he
says, "that the intention be something in the soul, a
sign naturally significatory of something for which it
can stand."[42] Few expressions occur more often in his
writings than that of a natural signification.

At this point it will be appropriate to outline the important distinction between the natural and conven-

[40] *Expositio aurea.* Praedicab. De Specie. In Prantl, op.
cit., vol. III, p. 332, Anm. 750.

[41] *Quodlib.* I, qu. 14, in Prantl, op. cit. Italics mine.

[42] *Summa tot. log.* I, 12, f. 6, r. B.

tional universal, which is a decisive factor in establishing the problem of Ockham's much discussed nominalism. In his own words: "the universal is twofold: natural and conventional. The first is a natural sign predicable of many things, as smoke naturally signifies fire, and a groan the pain of the sick man, and laughter a certain interior joy. The conventional universal is one by voluntary institution. Such is the spoken word which is an actual quality, numerically one, and universal because of its being a voluntarily instituted sign for the signification of many things."[43] Lothar Kugler, in his chapter "Ist Ockham Nominalist?"[44] discusses the complications of the problem of whether Ockham is a conceptualist or a nominalist and speaks of a conceptualistic-nominalism and of a nominalistic-conceptualism with great precision. My own position in this controversy is the following. By the very elusive name of nominalism I understand the view that regards concepts or terms as mere *subjective representations* for externally existing individual things. The words nominalism or terminism may be used interchangeably with the understanding that terminism emphasizes more the logico-propositional character of concepts. Concepts or terms are formulated in language symbols, the natural universal is clothed in the conventional universal. The more the vocalistic, grammatical element is emphasized, and the more universals are considered as common designations and collective names, the stricter, the more verbalistic is the nominalistic view. On the other hand, an emphasis put on the concept or intention of the soul considered as a universal mother-

43 *Sent.* II, qu. 25, P.

44 Lothar Kugler, *Der Begriff der Erkenntnis bei Wilhelm von Ockham,* Breslau, 1913, pp. 28-43.

tongue, results in what we call conceptualism, which is a mitigated form of nominalism.

What is Ockham's position in terms of these formulations? He sometimes implies the possibility of conceptual thinking without words; sometimes he seems to hold the view that concepts and words are inseparable. He distinguished spoken, written, and conceived propositions and says that "as we know the spoken proposition, we know just as truly the mental proposition which has no language."[45]   There is no doubt about the fact that the universal for him is basically a meaning, that is, a concept signifying naturally the members belonging under it.   Nevertheless he sometimes extends the name "universals" to the words designating these concepts.   The reason that he gives is that whatever is signified by the concept is signified concomitantly by the word as well, and *vice versa*.[46]   Yet he is anxious to add always that the word signifies by human decree (*institutio*),[47] while the concept signifies by nature.   Words are contrivances, concepts are natural products.[48]

To sum up, Ockham stresses the grammatical and verbal element enough to be called a genuine nominalist.   At the same time, the center of gravity of his theory of universals lies decidedly in the concept, which

[45] *Sent*. I, dist. 2, qu. 4, M.

[46] *Expos. aurea,* Praedicab., Proem., in Prantl, op. cit.

[47] *Summa tot. log.* I, 14, f. 6, v. B: "As the word is called common, the same also may be called universal, adding that this is not by the nature of the thing but only by the agreement of users."

[48] In *Quodlib*. IV. qu. 19, we read: "Et ista intentio secunda significat ita *naturaliter* intentiones primas et potest pro eis supponere in propositione, sicut intentio prima significat naturaliter res extra et potest pro eis supponere."   These words prove clearly how wrong Windelband is when he in his *A History of Philosophy,* New York, The Macmillan Co. 1923, p. 343, calls the "second intentions" arbitrary.

classifies him as a conceptualist. To combine both
views we may call him a nominalist of the vocalistic-
conceptualist type.

The nominalism of Ockham, however, will not be
set in its proper light until we see it as a terministic
nominalism. John Gerson (1363-1429), characterizing
the scholastic polemics of his time, names the two oppos-
ing parties as "formalistae" and "terministae."[49] By
designating the followers of Ockham as terminists he
gives us a good hint, for it is in the direction of terminism that we may find the most fruitful approach to
the discovery of the distinctive character of Ockham's
epistemology.

Prantl undoubtedly hit the nail on the head when he
summed up his laborious investigations concerning the
"Parteistellung" of Ockham in this sentence: "Die
principielle Unterordnung der Universalienfrage unter
den byzantinischen[50] Begriff 'terminus' ist die beson-
dere Eigentümlichkeit der Ansicht Occams's."[51] We
are familiar with the notion of *terminus* as being identical with any significatory intention, whenever it stands
in a proposition as subject or predicate. Why has this
notion such central significance in Ockham's epistemology? The reason will be quickly found if we remem-
ber that the essence of the universal lies in the notion
of predicability, that is, in the logical property of belonging to its *inferiora* by predication, by *dici de multis*.
Precisely because a universal signifies many individuals
and can be predicated of them, we call it a universal.
Direct signification, as when a first intention refers to

[49] Prantl, op. cit. IV, p. 146, Anm. 607, 613.

[50] Prantl's famous theory of "Byzantine logic," of course,
has been completely abandoned since the refutations of R.
Stapper, Ch. Thurot, and Valentine Rose.

[51] Prantl, op. cit. III, p. 344.

a class, does not give a universal. We need the reflecting act of predication to obtain the second intention or the universal. Predication, however, cannot
occur except in a logical proposition. Consequently,
the signifying intentions, in order to become universals, have to function as terms, that is, as parts of a
proposition. An intention of the soul, while it stands
outside of a proposition, signifies. When the same intention stands in a proposition, it becomes a term, and it
supposits. Because of the fact that the essence of the
universal lies in its predicability, the intention has to
function as a *terminus* in a proposition in order to become a universal. For that reason, second intentions are
never really mere intentions but always terms as well.[52]
Any intention, in order to become a universal, has to be
shifted from the psychological realm, i. e., from the
realm of mere signification, into the logical or proposi-
tional realm, i. e., into the realm of supposition. This
is the meaning of Prantl's statement subsuming Ockham's total doctrine of universals under the heading of
the *terminus*.

These discussions bring us back to our preliminary
statement that the whole epistemology and logic of Ockham centers around the two conceptions borrowed from
speculative grammar: signification and supposition.
The former is more an epistemological, the latter a
strictly logical conception. Let us clarify Ockham's
meaning concerning the latter.

He defines supposition in the following manner: By
supposition we mean the acceptance of terms for something else so that in a proposition we employ the term
for that something."[53] Expressed in a more modern

[52] *Sent.* I, dist. 23, qu. 1, D.

[53] *Summa tot. log.* I, 63, f. 20, v. B: "Dicitur autem suppositio, i. e., pro aliis positio, ita quod, quando terminus in propositione stat pro aliquo, utimur illo termino pro illo."

way in Überweg's *Grundriss*: "Die Supposition ist die Repräsentation dessen, was im Umfange eines Begriffes liegt, durch das diesen Begriff bezeichnende Wort."[54]   From the definition of Ockham it is clear that "the supposition is a property of the term yet never except in a proposition."[55]   *Supponere* is used by Ockham and in general by the scholastics in an intransitive sense, meaning to supposit, to substitute, to stand for, to represent vicariously.   The supposition is threefold: personal, simple, and material.   In a personal supposition we accept the terms of a proposition because they are signs of some really existing object.[56]   For instance, in the proposition "man is a rational animal," the term "man" stands for its signified objects, the individual men, and we accept and employ its supposition.   In a material supposition there is no signification but we accept the term for a word or a written symbol.   For instance in the proposition "man is a name," the term man supposits, stands for the word, and we accept and employ its substitution.[57]   The third type or simple supposition is historically of great significance because of its relation to the clash of realistic and nominalistic points of view.   Petrus Hispanus, the realist, differentiates the personal and simple supposition in the following manner: "The personal supposition is the acceptance of a general term for its *inferiora*.   The simple supposition is the acceptance of a term *for the universal thing* signified by the term itself."[58]   Now Ockham

[54] Friedrich Überweg, *Grundriss,* II, p. 578.

[55] *Summa tot. log.* I, 63, f. 20, v. B.

[56] *Summa tot. log.* C. 64, f. 21, r. A.

[57] *Summa tot. log.* C. 64, f. 21, r. A: "The material supposition is that in which the term does not function in a significative way, but stands either for the word or for a written sign."

[58] *Summulae logicales,* VII., in Prantl, op. cit., III, 51, Anm. 203-04.

could not use this definition because he eliminated the
res universalis from the ontological realm. The simple
supposition had to be reinterpreted according to his
epistemological criticism. The new, nominalistic definition was formulated this way: "The simple supposition is that in which the term stands for the intention
of the soul but not in a significative way."[59] The universal word, then, stands for nothing ontological, but
for psychological intentions. Signification, of course,
is excluded in a simple supposition, for nothing can be
a sign for itself. Ockham uses the following instance
for a simple supposition: "man is a species"; in this
proposition the term "man" stands for its own concept
and we accept and employ this substitution for the concept. This new definition of Ockham, although not
exactly a "facteur dissolvant de la synthese scholas-
tique," as Michalski puts it,[60] may surely be called a
symbol of the antagonism which was carried on between the *via antiqua,* the reales, and the *via moderna,*
the nominales, during the ensuing two hundred years.

A comparison of Ockham's notion of signification
with his notion of supposition makes it clear that the
former has a wider extent than the latter. Only the
personal supposition is based on signification, while the
simple and material suppositions are without any signification at all. The material supposition is restricted
to grammar. The simple supposition is used in rational
science or logic only. It is the personal supposition,
based on signification, and standing for external individual objects, that interests us most in our investigation
of how Ockham establishes the validity of knowledge.

[59] *Summa tot. log.* C. 64, f. 21, r. A.

[60] K. Michalski, *Les courants philosophiques à Oxford et à
Paris pendant le XIV-ème siecle,* 67.

Because the object of knowledge is to be found in universal propositions based on individuals, and the essence of any universal was discovered in its predicability or capacity to supposit for others, it is evident that Ockham's only way of building a bridge to the extramental world was to use the important property of his terms : supposition. It is because both the first and second intentions can supposit for individual objects that we can claim validity for our knowledge. The fact that the immediate subject-matter of any science is a proposition does not disturb the Venerabilis Inceptor. He knows that "although we speak of the thing, yet we speak of it by the intermediacy of propositions and terms."[61] He is well aware that in rational science these terms stand and supposit for intentions only. Yet he is firmly convinced that in real science propositions and terms stand and supposit for things.[62] This property of our terms is a sufficient guarantee for Ockham that our knowledge is not a mere subjective construction but can be validated in the objective world also. To express his idea in a different way, we may say that it is irrelevant for the spectroscopist whether the Frauenhofer lines are actually in the sun or are in the spectrum where we analyze them, taking it for granted all along that the spectral lines stand for solar and sidereal chemical elements. Frauenhofer's tomb bears the inscription, *Approximavit sidera;* the same phrase we may apply to Ockham, who did his best un-

[61] *Sent. I,* dist. 2, qu. 11, P.: "Quamvis loquimur de re, tamen loquimur de ea, mediante propositione et mediantibus terminis."

[62] *Sent.* II, dist. 2, qu. 4, C. N.: "Real science is distinguished from rational science in that the parts, that is, the terms of the known propositions in real science, stand and supposit for things, but not so the terms of the known propositions in rational science, where the terms stand and supposit for other things."

der the circumstances, and at least approximated reality by using his theory of supposition.

How Ockham uses supposition to establish the validity of knowledge can be best seen in his theory of truth. It is not necessary for a singular proposition, in order to be true materially, that the predicate should actually, *a parte rei,* inhere in the subject, but it is enough, if subject and predicate supposit, i. e., stand for, the same thing.[63] The case is the same with general propositions. In order to be true, the subject and predicate of a general proposition does not have to be one and the same actually in the order of things. It is enough if the predicate supposits, that is, stands for all that the subject stands for.[64]

To sum up, we have been investigating Ockham's theory of knowledge and its inseparable logical and metaphysical implications. We have been concentrating first on the mind-world relationship in its *psychological aspects* dealing with intentional signs. Our result was that psychologically the mind and the world are related to each other by the causal nexus of natural

[63] *Summa tot. log.* I, 2, c. 2: "To the truth of a singular proposition . . . it is not required that the subject and predicate be really the same, nor that the predicate be in the subject from the part of the thing, or to be really within the subject itself, nor that it be united to the subject itself from the part of the thing outside of the soul . . . but it is enough and is required, that the subject and predicate stand for the same thing. In these propositions: 'Socrates is a man,' 'Socrates is an animal,' . . . we denote that Socrates is really a man and is really an animal, not as if Socrates would be the predicate, animal or man, but in the sense that there is a thing for which this predicate 'man' and 'animal' stands and supposits, so that either of the two predicates stands for Socrates."

[64] *Summa tot. log.* I, 2. c. 4: "For the truth of a universal proposition it is not required that the subject and predicate be really the same, but it is required that the predicate should stand for all that the subject stands in order to be verified in them."

signification. In the second section, we have discussed the *logical aspects* of the mind-world relationship and have found that in Ockham's theory the validity of knowledge can be established logically by means of *supposition*.

These two properties of the terms: signification and supposition, indicate the remarkable bifurcation which we notice in Ockham's nominalistic philosophy. On one side, we are confronted with the most outspoken *empiricism,* on the other, with a logical *formalism*.

The first trend develops from the idea of *signification*. Reality is pluralistic and individual. Its causal influences result in mental signs, that is, in concrete first intentions which signify their sources of origin. The universal in its psychological being is an act of intellect which naturally signifies the particular objects belonging to it. There is no other universal or common nature in things. Essence and existence coincide. There is no need for any principle of individuation, because there is no common essence to be individualized.[65] Reality in its inmost being is concrete and individual. We formulate and systematize this reality in the real sciences, consisting of propositions, the terms of which stand, by means of personal supposition for concrete individuals on the basis of natural signification.

The second trend develops along the idea of *supposition*. Because of the elimination of the ontological universal, terms of the second intention such as *species, genus, differentia,* etc., do not signify anything in the external world. Such terms in propositions can sup-

[65] *Sent.* I, dist. 2, qu. 6, P: "Any particular thing is singular as it is . . . therefore, whatever is singular without adding something to it is singular by itself.

posit and stand only for their own intentions, that is, admit of only simple supposition. Terms employed in simple supposition were thus cut off from the external world and had to develop in isolation. Their function was restricted to the working out of rules that establish relations between conceptions. The *scientia rationalis,* or logic, with the exclusive use of the *suppositio simplex,* turned into a strictly formalistic *scientia sermocinalis,* which by an exclusive cultivation of the rules of formal relations left any other problem to the metaphysician.[66]

Another important bifurcation was created by Ockham's epistemological dualism between the external world and its representation in the mind. With his theory of signs, he inserted a medium between the knowing mind and the knowable world in such a way that what had been for ages a *means* of knowledge, became with him the immediate *object* of knowledge. The setting of the problem of knowledge in this manner became of immeasurable importance for the coming centuries. Ockham's nominalistic formulations, so rich in their implications, contained the seeds of the entire problem of knowledge which was to dominate later centuries of European philosophy.

[66] *Sent.* I, dist. 23, qu. 1, D: "Whether the second intentions are really and psychologically or only logically in the soul, has no reference to the problem and it is not up to the logician to determine. The logician's principal task is to consider the distinction between the terms of the first and second intentions. What the logician precisely is expected to say is that in this proposition 'man is a species' the subject stands for a common something and not for something which it signifies. Whether that common something is real or not real is none of his, but the metaphysician's business."

OCKHAM'S NATURAL PHILOSOPHY

OCKHAM'S natural philosophy is sealed with seven seals. Very little is known about it yet. Except for a few articles[1] and the splendid but short and only fragmentary presentation of Dr. Simon Moser,[2] published in 1932, nothing has yet been written on this very interesting part of his doctrine. The very titles of his books on this subject are hard to collect. The only sources available are Andrew G. Little[3] and Dr. Ludwig Baur.[4]

The first book dealing with natural philosophy is listed by Little under the title *Quaestiones in octo libros physicorum. Incipit "Valde reprehensibilis videtur, qui. . ."* Dr. Baur quotes the book as *Quaestiones in libros Physicorum* with the *Incipit "Utrum privatio sit aliqua res."* The manuscript is in Merton College, Oxford. While Little gives only two printed publications, one in Strassburg, 1491, and the other one in Rome, 1637, Dr. Baur knows about another Strassburg publication in 1506 and one printed the same year in Venice.

The second book has not been printed and can be

---

[1] P. Duhem, "Le temps et le mouvement selon les scolastiques," *Revue de Philosophie,* 14, (1914). P. Doncoeur, "La théorie de la matière et de la forme chez Guillaume d'Occam, *R. ScPh. Th.,* 10, (1921), 21-51.

[2] Dr. Simon Moser, *Grundbegriffe der Naturphilosophie bei Wilhelm von Ockham,* Innsbruck, 1932.

[3] Andrew G. Little, *The Grey Friars in Oxford,* Oxford, 1892.

[4] Dr. Ludwig Baur, "Die philosophischen Werke des Robert Grosseteste," *Beiträge zur Geschichte der Philosophie des Mittelalters* (hereafter to be quoted as *BGPM*) 1912, 124*, 1 (wrongly quoted by De Wulf in the second volume of his *History of Medieval Philosophy,* p. 186, as *BGPM* XVIII, 4-6).

seen in Brussels in a manuscript, numbered 469, and dating from the fourteenth century. Little quotes the work under the title *Quaestiones Ockam super phisicam et tractatus ejusdam de futuris contingentibus.* Dr. Baur mentions this work under the title *Super libros physicorum* with the *Incipit "Valde reprehensibilis videtur, qui . . ."* and gives the manuscript as Merton 293, Oxford. It seems that Baur mixes up the *Incipit* of this manuscript with that of the first book.

The only book of which the title is settled is the third one. Both Little and Baur agree by quoting it as *Summulae in libros physicorum.* The first edition of this book was printed at Bologna in 1494, the second at Venice in 1506 (Baur wrongly says 1508), the last in Rome, 1637.

These three books, however, do not complete the list of Ockham's books on Natural Philosophy. Little mentions another work ascribed to Ockham and preserved at Assisi, which he thinks may be there still. *Incipit prologus:* "*Philosophos plurimos.*" *Incipit opus:* "*Iste liber dividitur in duas partes.*" Duhem, in his aforementioned article, makes abundant quotations from another work of Ockham entitled *De successivis. Incipit:* "*Videndum est de locis.*" We have two manuscripts of this work, one in Paris in the Bibliothèque Nationale 16130, f. 121 (sec. XIV); another one in Brussels numbered 500. And if we may follow the lead of the title, in Ockham's *De motu, loco, tempore, relatione, praedestinatione et praescientia Dei et quodlibetum,* we may find material concerning our subject. This last work is extant in one manuscript in Basel, f. 11, 24, and in several others in Paris in the Bibliothèque Nationale.

Baur's comprehensive statement[5] with reference to all these works is that their authenticity and mutual relationship has yet to be established. Until this can be done we have to rely on the only accessible and undoubtedly authentic sources of the *Summulae in libros physicorum*,[6] and the Commentary to the *Sentences,* to reconstruct a scheme of Ockham's natural philosophy. The quotations which follow are taken from the second edition of the *Summulae,* printed in 1506 in Venice, and from the 1495 Lyons edition of the Commentary to the *Sentences.*

William of Ockham's natural philosophy is to be studied in the light of his Aristotelian empiricism. The very fact that he, interested always in the concrete and individual, wrote on natural philosophy at all is an outcome of his empirical trend of mind. This basically "earth-bound" inclination comes even more into prominence when we consider the treatment of single problems. The following pages will give ample proof of a typically positivistic way of tackling problems. The famous razor (*frustra fit per plura quod potest fieri per pauciora*) is always in readiness to cut out imaginary, supersensuous, or occult elements from physical problems. Nothing really matters to him but that which can be experienced. His main effort consists in simplifying situations and in reducing complicated questions to a few elementary propositions. This general methodology leaves no doubt that, although very often opposed to particular Aristotelian views, Ock-

[5] Op. cit., ". . . deren Echtheit und gegenseitiges Verhältnis noch der Untersuchung harrt."

[6] Moser, Op. cit., p. 5: As to the other printed books of Ockham on Natural Philosophy, Dr. Moser writes: "Ich konnte trotz mehrerer Anfragen bei massgebenden Stellen den Standort der *Quaestiones in octo libros physicorum* (Argentor. 1491) nicht ermitteln."

ham's natural philosophy is an eloquent manifestation
of what is most distinctive in Aristotelianism: the empirical spirit.

Instead of attempting the impossible task of giving
a comprehensive presentation of Ockham's philosophy
of nature, we will select some outstanding and typical
doctrines in which the empirical treatment is most obvious and which have most influenced posterity.

Let us investigate first Ockham's treatment of hylo-
morphism—that is, his interpretation of matter and
form.

As natural science deals with composite physical
bodies, one of its chief tasks is to investigate the principles and causes of this composition: matter and form.
Ockham proves the existence of both *a posteriori*. We
see that things are in process, they come into existence
and disappear. Now no thing can be generated out of
nothing. In all process there must be something presupposed. This *praesuppositum* must be in the thing as
a necessary constituent of the natural product. We call
this matter. The other constituent which is just as
necessary, although not presupposed, is the form.[7]

Ockham, by accepting these basic notions of the peri-
patetic philosophy, loses no time in transforming them
according to his nominalistic criticism. Matter and
form as universals do not exist except in the mind.
When, therefore, we say that every physical body is
composed of matter and form we should think of a
particular matter and a particular form. The thesis
that "there are only two principles underlying every
generation,"[8] is false, but we may say that "every
generation and every generated product has only two

[7] William of Ockham, *Summulae in libros Physicorum,* I, 7.
[8] *Summulae,* I, 14: "Tantum duo sunt principia cuiuslibet
generationis."

principles."[9] Although Ockham thinks that Aristotle agrees with him and quotes from the *Metaphysics* that "no universal is a substance"[10] and that, therefore, no universal is by itself the principle of something singular, we know that in the *Metaphysics* of Aristotle the μορφή is identical with the εἶδος, which is universal for the Philosopher.[11] In Ockham's contention the form is not a *praesuppositum,* but becomes existent precisely through and in the process of generation.[12] This emphasis on the concrete character of all matter and form is a definite advancement beyond the empiricism of Aristotle.

What, now, is Ockham's view about matter and form, considered, not as constituents of a composite, but in themselves? Concerning matter he shares the Aristotelian distinction of second and first matter. First matter (*materia prima*), or primordial stuff, is the very first formless element which is capable of receiving any possible form (*forma substantialis*) and out of which thereby various other or second matters are constituted until we reach the *materia ultima,* that is, the matter of the body under consideration. On closer investigation we will find that Aristotle's conception of first matter, strictly followed by Saint Thomas Aquinas, is quite different from that of the Venerabilis Inceptor. While with Aristotle and Thomas Aquinas first matter is a sheer potentiality, Ockham defines the same in the following manner: "Matter is a certain

[9] *Sumulae,* I, 14.

[10] Aristotle, *Metaphysics,* VII, 8, Oxford: Clarendon Press, 1908. "Nullum universale est substantia."

[11] *Metaphysics,* I, 7; 190 b 20 and 28.

[12] *Summulae,* I, 14: "Although first matter which is a first principle precedes the generated product, yet the form which is a first principle does not precede the generated product, but has its existence by generation (habet esse per generationem)."

thing which actually exists in the nature of things, being in potentiality to all substantial forms although not
necessarily having any . . . And therefore, matter is not
to be visualized as something by itself only in potentiality which is to be actualized in such and such a
manner.   Matter is really actual by itself and it can
by no means be reduced to a mere potentiality.   It is
always actual in the nature of things although always
in potentiality with reference to the form which it
lacks."[13]   He proves this actual character of first matter by pointing out that anything that is not *in actu,*
but only can be so, could be produced and begin to be.
Matter, however, should not be visualized in such manner, for then it could not underlie all process.   Consequently, it must be always actual.   With this belief that
first matter never can begin to exist, Ockham clearly
clashes with the Catholic dogma according to which
whatever exists was created in time.

The doctrine of the actual character of first matter
is of ancient origin.   It goes back as far as Plato's notion of the χώρα, developed in the *Timaeus* (50, b),
as the underlying substratum of all cosmic process.   It
is formless, yet real.   This doctrine, so foreign to the
Christian notion of creation, infiltrated into the West
through three channels.   The first was the *Timaeus* itself, the only Platonic writing known to the early Middle Ages (in the translation of Cicero and the Christian Chalcidius).   The second was Saint Augustine,
who clearly adopts a casually, though not temporally,
preëxistent actual matter.[14]   The third was Gebirol, the

[13] *Summulae,* I, 15.

[14] Augustine, *In Genesim ad Lit.,* Lib. V, cap. 5, Migne, P.
L., vol. 34, col. 326: "Non temporali sed causali ordine prius
facta est informis formabilisque materies, et spiritualis et cor-
poralis, de qua fieret quod faciendum esset."

Jewish philosopher, also called Avicebron or Avence-
brol, whose doctrine of *materia universalis* developed in
his *Fons Vitae,* exerted a tremendous influence on the
Scholastics from Gundisalvi up to Duns Scotus, who
openly subscribes to Gebirol's doctrine of matter.[15]   It
may be said that in general all the representatives of
Augustinism were unanimous in accepting in one sense
or another an actual first matter.

The danger which Ockham had to face in interpret-
ing matter as actual, lay in the possibility of his slipping
into monism. Duns Scotus, himself, by recourse to the
materia universalis of Gebirol which is common in
everything, and utilizing it in his *materia primo prima,*
was walking on the verge of monism. Nothing could be
farther from the mode of thought of Ockham.   He,
therefore, takes the greatest precautions to sail safely
between the Scylla of monism and the Charybdis of
sensualistic pluralism. He allows the unitary character
of first matter, but only in so far as it has the same
potentiality to receive possible substantial forms. Nevertheless, as actual, first matter is numerically distinct
and different in every existent,[16] so that he can say
"my own first matter is one thing, your first matter is
another,"[17] which is precisely the opinion of another

[15] Duns Scotus, *De Rerum Principio,* qu. VIII, art. 4, n. 24:
"Avicebron in libro Fons Vitae dixit unam in omnibus esse
materiam, . . . Ego autem ad positionem Avicembronis redeo."
As against the denial of the authenticity of this work of Scotus by E. Longpré in his *La Philosophie du B. Duns Scot.*
(1924) 16-49, 288-91, the writer is inclined to accept the view
of C. R. S. Harris in his *Duns Scotus* (Oxford, 1927), vol. I,
pp. 364-75, which accepts it as authentic.
[16] *Summulae,* I, 18: "Materia prima est eiusdem rationis in
omnibus compositis, sed non una numero in omnibus compositis;
immo in omnibus generatis simul existentibus sunt diversae
materiae primae numero distinctae vel differentes, quomodo
diversae albedines differunt."
[17] *Summulae,* I, 14: "Alia est materia prima mea et alia est
prima materia tua."

great empiricist and believer in the actuality of first matter, Roger Bacon.[18]

We will end this discussion of Ockham's theory of matter by pointing out one more aspect of his doctrine, which was to become of great historical importance. Ockham adds the following description of matter: "It is impossible to have first matter without extension, for matter cannot exist without having parts distant from part. But this is tantamount to saying that matter is extended, is quantitative and dimensionate; for dimension, quantity, and extension are nothing else than the distance of one part from the other."[19] A full appreciation of this conception will be possible only in a later part of this discussion.

Turning to Ockham's conception of form, we are confronted again with his typical approach. This time his positivistic tendency turns into a sort of agnosticism. Using an *a posteriori* argument, he comes to the conclusion that we need to assume the existence of form. In every natural generation and corruption there is a part which is new. This new something cannot be matter, for matter is a substance which is never generated nor corrupted. Therefore, it must be the form[20] As to how form and matter are the principles of generation, we get a very unscholastic answer. "Matter and form," we hear, "are simultaneously in the same place and position so that form presupposes matter and is received by it."[21]

Ockham is seemingly in a very difficult position. He

[18] J. S. Brewer, *Fr. Rogeri Bacon Opera quaedam hactenus inedita*, (Londinii, 1859), p. 126: "Forma differt a forma secundum se, et materia per suas naturas proprias, ita quod diversitas materiae non est a forma sicut nec a converso."

[19] *Summulae,* I, 14.

[20] *Summulae,* I, 21.

[21] *Summulae,* I, 23.

is using the conception of form without its Aristotelian meaning. For Aristotle, the form was the universal essence which became actualized into the individual. Ockham rejected the ontological universal with its formal causation. What was he to do with a conception thus enervated? How was he to account for individuation without even the Scotist *"haecceitas,"* which he rejected? We see him taking a strictly positivistic stand with the outlook of an agnostic on the situation.

He makes an insignificant observation by saying that form, the new element in becoming (*quae de novo recipitur* and *fit de novo*) "is not of the same 'ratio' in generated products," thereby differing from matter, "which is of the same 'ratio' in all things."[22] But we are more anxious to know how that new something is originated. Is it created? Where does it come from? Ockham's answer is that it is brought forth by "natural agents." Yet, he does not settle the question of how natural agents possess the power to produce forms. Instead he surprises us by telling that 'form is extended, having parts distant from part."[23] This is typical of his thinking fixed always on the phenomenal and positivistic rather than on the hidden and metaphysical. Form is, of course, the finished and apparent result of a formal activity too, and as such is extended. But what about the formal causality? Ockham's definition of the formal cause gives some indication of an answer when he describes it as a "distinct thing which informs matter."[24] As to what informing means, we find it explained in terms of potentiality and act. 'Matter is some potentiality destined to receive that form,

22 *Summulae,* I, 21.
23 *Summulae,* I, 21.
24 *Summulae,* II, 2.

and form is some act destined to be received in that matter."[25]   Does this answer solve our problem of what form really is?

Ockham knows that positivistically he is not able to obtain more definite results. He stops short, therefore, and confesses in all honesty his ignorance. "And if it is asked why matter is potentiality and form is act, the answer is that such is the nature of the thing and there is no other cause for it but that matter is matter and form is form. To be sure, this is no proper cause, and, therefore, we have no proper cause here. To the rejoinder that since no cause can be assigned here, we should not introduce anything without necessity and cause, the answer is that on the basis of experience or reason many things are to be introduced that have no causes . . . And this happens either because they have no causes or they have such but we do not know them, as in the present case. Reason and experience prompt us to introduce matter and form as concurring to the constitution of composite things so that from the potentiality of matter the form is being brought forth as its act."[26]

This is the most that can be said of Ockham's notion of form, a view which places him in a strange intermediary position between the ancient doctrine and the yet distant dawn of the notion of force which was to supplant that of form.

Inasmuch as we gained the conception of matter and form by investigating generation, which is mutation and motion, our next task will be to expound Ockham's conception of motion.

True to his own genius he approaches this topic, too,

[25] *Summulae,* 1, 23.
[26] *Summulae,* I, 23.

in his typically positivistic manner. He controverts Aristotle's notion according to which motion, κίνησις, is a certain kind of flux, a transition from potentiality, δύναμις, to actuality, ἐντελέχεια.[27] He interprets the definition in a twofold manner. In one sense, it may mean that motion is a thing distinct from all permanent things, flowing continuously from non-being to being; in the other sense, it may mean that one part of being continuously passes, another continuously succeeds in the nature of things.[28]

Against this definition he sets up his basic view that "bodies moving in space do not acquire anything inherent."[29] His thesis is that there is no difference whatever between the thing that moves, the *"res permanens,"* and motion identified with some *"forma transiens,"* but that "the moving body itself is the motion itself on its own account."[30]

He proves his thesis by arguments taken from the nature of change in general. To change means to be in a state different from the previous one. For this it is sufficient to have permanent things so that one is in the place of the other when the former is not there, or that one is not present where it was before. In order to bring about darkness in a light room we do not need any transient something to be destroyed successively as one instant follows the other, but it is enough that by the removal of the cause of light the form of darkness supplants the form of light. To quote Ockham: "When a thing changes into a form

[27] Aristotle, *Physics,* Berlin edition, III, 1, 200, 10-11.

[28] *Summulae* III, 7: "This is the far-famed way of conceiving motion which I think represents the notion of the Philosopher and the Commentator (i. e. Averroes)."

[29] Ibid.

[30] *Sent.* II, qu. 26, M: "Ideo dico ipsum movens . . . est ipsum motum secundum se."

which it did not have before, it is not necessary to suppose two forms: a permanent and a transient. A
single form which was not there before is adequate to
explain the notion of change. There is no need to
posit transient things besides the permanent things
which endure through time."[31]

What he established for change in general, he ap-
plies to any sort of motion. If motion actually were
some absolute thing inherent in the body that moves,
it would have to be either substance or quantity. In
that case, however, when a thing moved, it would swell
or diminish its quantity which is absurd. Much less
could it be a quality or a relation. Consequently, motion cannot be a thing that inheres as a transient something.[32]

Having discarded the "occult" element in motion,
Ockham finds it much harder to explain what *motion*
really is. He gives his view in a very concise manner:
"For the concept of motion it is sufficient that the body
in question move continuously, without being inter-
rupted by time or rest, one state succeeding another
with no break."[33] He thinks that in local motion we do
not need anything besides the mobile body itself that
continuously and successively occupies diverse places.

Will such a purely descriptive explanation satisfy
his adversaries? Ockham anticipates their reply that
no body moves unless it acquires something which it
did not have before. In his answer he cleverly de-
clines to be allured into metaphysical regions and sticks
solidly to his phenomenological ground. "Of course,
it has something new," he replies, "yet, nothing sub-

[31] *Summulae,* III, 3.
[32] *Summulae,* III, 5.
[33] *Summulae,* III, 6.

stantially inherent, but it has acquired a different location. And if you further inquire as to what is necessary for the body to be in that place, I reply that nothing else is required but a body and a place and the absence of any intermediary moving in one or another direction."[34] He is so emphatic at this point that if he could, he would even eliminate certain confusing words from the dictionary introduced there by the figurative language of Aristotle and Averroes.[35] "If we sought precision," we hear the Venerabilis Inceptor say, "by using words like 'mover,' 'moved,' 'movable,' and the like, instead of words like 'motion,' 'mobility,' and others of the kind, many difficulties and doubts would be excluded."[36]

How definite Ockham is in his view may be seen in the case of projectile motion. What is the impelling principle of a projected stone? It seems that Ockham will hardly be able to refuse some force as an efficient principle impressed upon the moving body. Überweg makes the mistake of identifying Ockham with the theory of impetus maintained by John Buridan (d. after 1358) and the whole Parisian physicist school of the fourteenth century.[37] The fact is that Ockham unflinchingly kept his ground and rejected any impetus in the projected stone. Another instance in which Ockham again eliminates any element of inherent force is when he deals with the action at a distance. In his opinion the magnet attracts the iron which is spatially distant from it not by virtue of something existing in the intermediary space or in the iron, but directly and

[34] *Summulae,* III, 7.
[35] *Summulae,* I, 13: "Aristoteles et Averroes frequenter utuntur sermonibus impropriis et figurativis et tropicis."
[36] *Summulae,* III, 7.
[37] Überweg, op. cit., II, 597.

through the distance without utilizing a medium.[38]

Ockham's conception of motion is one of his views which is most out of harmony with doctrines of the time. It stood in diametrical opposition to the Aristotelian view maintained by such men of his age as Averroes, Roger Bacon, Albert the Great, Thomas Aquinas, Peter d'Auvergne (d. 1304), Giles of Rome (1247-1316), Walter Burley (d. after 1343), John of Jandun (d. 1328), and generally by the whole chorus of thirteenth-century physicists. The thesis that "the thing moving and the movement are thoroughly indistinguishable"[39] was generally rejected by even the nominalists of the Parisian school of physicists and did not find understanding up to the beginning of the modern era.

"Because time is motion or something belonging to motion," so the fourth part of the *Summulae* begins, "after motion we have to investigate time."[40] Ockham's approach is the same as in the case of movement. First, he wants to establish what instant and time are not, by eliminating any uncontrollable element. Apparently arguing against Thomas Aquinas, he asserts that the instant is not a fluent entity, appearing and disappearing so that always a new instant comes to sight successively which is to be distinguished from permanent things. His proof is another application of his law of parsimony: *frustra fit per plura quod potest fieri per pauciora.* The *primum mobile,* that is, the sphere of the fixed stars, can move locally without acquiring any other thing, and account fully in itself for time. Therefore, it is superfluous to assume such a thing as an indivisible instant distinguished from per-

[38] *Sent.* II, qu. 18, E.
[39] *Sent.* II, qu. 26, M.
[40] *Summulae,* IV, 1.

manent things.[41]   In the same way, he rejects the view
that time considered in its wholeness (*secundum se
totam*) would be something different from the permanent things.   Time in that case ought to be either substance or quality, neither of which is distinguished from
permanent things.[42]

Ockham's next task is to explain what time is. Time,
in his view, is the measure of three things: of motion,
of temporal things with different duration, and of rest.
In order to be able to measure we have to know the
quantity of the measure more than the quantity of the
thing to be measured. "Time is not a latent, unknowable thing,"[43] it is a thing *notum valde*.[44]   Time is that
something whereby we are rendered certain (*certifica-
mur*) about the duration of temporal things, motions
and rest.   Consequently, his definition of time: "Time
is the measure of all things the duration of which can
be established by the intellect by means of something
better known."[45]

With an allusion to Aristotle's definition of time,
according to which "time is the numbered motion with
reference to the former and latter,"[46] Ockham points
out the close connection between motion and time. By
numbering and measuring the uniformity of motion
we can measure time, although we cannot attribute the
notion of time to any motion. When somebody ascer-
tains the hour of the day and the position of the sun

[41] *Summulae,* IV, 1.

[42] *Summulae,* IV, 2.

[43] *Summulae,* IV, 3.

[44] Newton expresses himself in the same way: "tempus, spa-
tium, locum et motum ut omnibus notissima non definio . . ."
Philosophiae naturalis principia mathematica, def. 8, quoted
in Moser, op. cit., p. 169.

[45] *Summulae,* IV, 3.

[46] *Phys.* II, IV, 11; 219 b, 1-2.

on the sky by his own movement and daily routine (*exercitium*), his movements cannot be called time.

As to the question how time exists, we read the following sentence. "The short proposition: time is, is an abridgement for this longer one: A mobile thing moves uniformly while the intellect considers and numbers its passage before it arrives at a certain place and then while it is there and afterwards while it is somewhere else, so that the intellect can thereby ascertain for how long other things perdure or move or rest."[47] This descriptive definition brings out clearly that properly speaking time should be attributed only to the first motion of the first mobile thing, that is, to the Ptolemaic sphere of the fixed stars as it rapidly and uniformly turns around the earth. Even the motion of the sun and the planets (*motus inferiori*) are measured by this normative motion. This ontological character of time is quite strong in Ockham's conception. Time for him is the passion of the first motion, or rather the first motion itself. He identifies the instant, too, with the *primum mobile*. "The instant is nothing else than the first mobile thing existing somewhere according to its parts where it was not immediately before and will not be immediately after."[48] Accordingly, the instant varies its position because the "now" is pronounced successively at various places.

So far Ockham's view is not different from that of Aristotle. The philosopher, too, conceives of time as ontologically dependent upon motion, as a πάθος or property of motion essentially residing in it and not something only accidental to it. In his view, wherever there is motion there is time, and vice versa, the eter-

[47] *Summulae,* IV, 5.
[48] *Summulae,* IV, 8.

nity of time implying the eternity of motion.

The distinctive feature of Ockham's conception lies in his subjectivistic approach. Motion is not an absolute measure, for, as we shall see presently, it involves an aspect of the soul. Time is a measure only in so far as we compare the movement of the sphere of the fixed stars and the motion of the body in question. The relation of these two motions will give time. In Ockham's words: "If we observe that *a* was moving while the *primum mobile* moved from east to west, and *b* was moving only while the *primum mobile* moved from east to the zenith, we may know that *a* moved for a longer time than *b*."[49] Strangely, the question how we can know the movement of the *primum mobile* never arises in the mind of the Venerabilis Inceptor. He is satisfied to know that its motion is uniform and the fastest. For practical purposes, of course, we may use the *motus inferiores,* for instance, our own movements, to measure the location of the sun or the hour-glass to know how much the *primum mobile* or the sun moved, but this is not a certain way of measuring, nor one following from the nature of the thing.

It seems that Ockham differentiates an ideal and a practical time, in a manner somewhat similar to Newton's absolute and relative time.[50] He is certain, however, that for both, the measuring activity of the soul is essential. Unless somebody realizes that the uniformly moving *primum mobile* first is in one place and afterwards in another, he can never perceive time. In

[49] *Summulae,* IV, 14.

[50] Newton, *Philosophiae naturalis principia mathematica,* Genevae 1739; in Moser, op. cit., p. 170: "Tempus absolutum, verum et mathematicum, in se et natura sua sine relatione ad externum quodvis aequabiliter fluit, alioque nomine dicitur Duratio; relativum, apparens et vulgare est sensibilis et externa quaevis Durationis per motum mensura."

his own words: "No matter how uniform and fast the first motion is, unless there is a soul, that motion can not be time,"[51] or to put it in a more emphatic way: *Si anima non posset esse, tempus esse non posset.*[52] The rod which in reality is an ell (or yard) could not be an ell if the soul did not exist, for without the soul nothing could be measured by the rod.[53]

The objective and subjective character of time is explained by a fine distinction. Time may be taken in a twofold sense. In the one, time is that whereby the soul is rendered certain.[54] In the other, time is that by which the soul can be rendered certain about other things.[55] In the first sense, it is true that if the soul did not number the first motion, there would be no time. In the second sense, the first motion is time whether the soul measures it or not, although for actual time we always need the soul. Ockham accepts this more objective time on the basis that the common people would find it strange to hear that there is no time without the soul. As a matter of fact, of course, soul and time are inseparable.[56] To use an illustration, the cause does not depend on its effect, yet the cause cannot be without its effect.[57]

Ockham's conception of time, far from having any particular relationship to Kant, is much nearer the notion of Newton, who liked to characterize time as quan-

[51] *Summulae,* IV, 14.

[52] Moser, op. cit., p. 165. In the text of the *Summulae,* IV, 16: "Si anima non posset esse tempus non posset esse tempus."
[53] Ibid.

[54] *Summulae,* IV, 16: "Tempus est illud per quod anima certificatur."

[55] Ibid.: "Tempus est illud per quod anima potest certificari de aliis."

[56] *Summulae,* IV, 7: "Tempus importat animam."

[57] *Summulæ,* IV, 16.

tity.[58] Ockham, with his strong insistence on the quantitative *res permanentes,* based time on the motion of permanent things. At the same time, Ockham emphatically points out the rôle of the soul as well. In fact, precisely at this point does he differ from Aristotle and Thomas Aquinas. The idea, however, that makes the cooperation of the soul indispensable is that of measuring.[59] Thus, both the quantitative and mathematical aspects are united in his conception, pointing in the direction of seventeenth-century science.

The idea of motion and time introduces the problem of infinity. Beginning with his quantitative notion of permanent things, Ockham sets up his thesis of the possibility of infinite diminution and infinite augmentation. His contention is that no matter how small a given particle may be, divine power could always produce a smaller one, and no matter how large a quantity may be, God always could add to it. Aristotle, with his idea of a finite universe, restricted such augmentation. The Philosopher thinks that it would be a contradiction to assume the increase of water filling the sphere. Ockham daringly replies that God could make another world, or even an infinite number of worlds.

Ockham's notion of infinity, however, excludes the actual realization of the infinitely small or infinitely large. He makes a fine distinction by denying the possibility of the infinitely small or large *in fact* (*in facto esse*), and admitting only the possibility of the infinite *in becoming* (*in fieri*). Any reduction of the datum to such actuality as to exclude any further pos-

[58] Newton, op. cit., Def. 7, Scholium, in Moser, op. cit. p. 167.
[59] *Summulae,* IV, 16: "Mensura in sua definitione respicit animam."

sibility of diminution or augmentation frustrates the very notion of the infinite and turns it *eo ipso* into a finite datum. We never can attain to the infinite *in fact* that has realized in actuality all that was in potentiality. Potentialities for new becoming never can be exhausted.

Ockham's idea of the possibility of infinite process (which he always connects with the creative power of God), constitutes one of his truly admirable contributions. It is an intellectual intuition reaching into the very structure of the universe, keenly sensitive to its inexhaustible and emerging nature, which, instead of ever coming to a standstill is continuous in endless creativity. Perhaps it is not too much to say that we may recognize in Ockham's doctrine of an infinite progress toward the infinitely small which always results in a finite structure, a dim presentiment of the infinitesimal calculus, later more distinctly felt by Nicholas of Cusa and brought to fruition by Newton and Leibniz.

An extension of Ockham's views on the possibility of infinite process led to his doctrine of the possible plurality of worlds. This doctrine was also in opposition to the views of his age, which firmly stood on the Aristotelian teaching of the impossibility of more than one world. Aristotle's argument was that another world would either move toward our earth, that is the center of our world, or would not. If it would, it would be a part of our world; if it would not, we would have to accept the absurdity that certain heavy bodies move away from our earth. Ockham answers that bodies in a different world should just as little move toward the center of our world, as a fire going up at Oxford would move toward one and the same place as if it were at Paris.[60]

Ockham's doctrine of the plurality of worlds was to find its full development in Giordano Bruno's book, *De l'infinito, universo e mondi,* in which his famous doctrine of the infinity of the worlds was developed.

These considerations bring us to another interesting view of Ockham: that of the homogeneousness of the universe. The medievals, following Averroes' views, taught that the material of celestial bodies has nothing in common with the earthly elements. Thomas Aquinas rejects Averroes' view of heaven as a pure form and admits matter in the celestial substance, a matter which, in his view, however, is so different in nature that it can be mentioned with our earthly matter only in terms of analogy.[61]

William of Ockham, following Duns Scotus, who greatly minimized the heterogeneousness of heavenly and earthly matter, categorically states that both the heavenly and lower bodies are formed out of the very same material and are, therefore, homogeneous. His proofs are merely speculative but at least he has the honesty not to claim any demonstrative force for them. At the same time he cannot see how the opposite view could be proven.[62]

Ockham's view was generally rejected by the scholastics of his age. Even the Parisian nominalists and physicists found this view too daring, and led by Albert of Saxony (d. 1390) discarded it. Ockham's

[60] *Sent.* I, dist. 44, F.

[61] Pierre Duhem, *Études sur Leonard da Vinci,* Paris, 1909, II, p. 250.

[62] *Sent.* II, qu. 22, D: "Dico quod in celestibus et in istis inferioribus est materia eiusdem rationis omnino, licet haec pars non possit demonstrari sic, nec alia tamen potest persuaderi."

healthy empirical instinct, however, found the right direction. After a century or so, Nicolaus Cusanus (1401-1464) adopted the same view which was to be later established by modern astrophysics.

This abridged presentation of Ockham's natural philosophy is intended to be an illustration of his empirical spirit. It is hoped that the particular doctrines which have been brought forth served this purpose. To sum up we may state that Ockham's method is positivistic throughout. He betrays a certain aversion toward non-phenomenal, transient, fluent, latent entities in connection with the questions considered. His chief concern is to reduce problems from imaginary levels to simple, sensory data, just as he is eager to reduce figures of speech to distinct and clear expressions.

Historically, the most significant mark of Ockham's natural philosophy is his concentration on the permanent thing. In the midst of the qualitative dynamism of generation, mutation, and motion, his eyes do not seem to notice anything except the static, extended, and quantitative thing. While he devotes, in his *Summulae,* numerous chapters to matter, he gives only a brief consideration to form. In investigating first matter, he treats it as something actual and extended, and he attributes the same character to form. When he comes to the problem of motion, instead of giving an explanation of the essence of movement as such, he treats of motion as a change of spatial positions. All along the succeeding stages of motion it is the permanent thing which interests him; in fact, motion is nothing but the permanent thing considered in different locations. Even in the motion of projectiles he eliminates anything but

the moving body as being the motion itself.[63]   The
same tendency for spatialization may be observed in
his doctrine of time. Time for Ockham is a process of
measuring changing locations in terms of the normative
motion of the sphere of the fixed stars. Here we see
again the tendency to consider in changing bodies the
quantitative, the measurable and the mathematical.

Ockham's natural philosophy, with its emphasis on
the permanent thing which is extended, quantitative
and measurable, may be looked upon as an early prel-
ude to seventeenth-century natural science, and a fore-
runner of the mathematico-mechanical world-view of
Descartes and Newton; while Ockham's speculations
on the possibility of infinite process and the plurality
of worlds found their continuation in the imaginative
naturalism of the Renaissance.

At this point attention may be called to the startling
statements of Pierre Duhem, outstanding historian of
Physics and Cosmology, who in his writings created a
sensation by pointing out the Parisian Ockhamist school
in the fourteenth century as the earliest starting point
of our modern scientific era. In his *Études sur Léonard de Vinci,* (Paris, 1909) Duhem introduces Ockham as the moving spirit of this scientific center and
links up his name with some of the greatest achieve-
ments of modern science. In his own words: "Auda-
cious opponent of Aristotle as he was, Ockham appears
to us sometimes as a precursor of Descartes, sometimes as a precursor of Newton. The propositions
which he formulated seem to us today strangely

[63] *Sent.* II, qu. 26, M: "Ideo dico ipsum movens in tali
motu post separationem mobilis a primo projiciente est ipsum
motum secundum se . . . ita quod movens et motum est penitus
indistinctum."

prophetic."[64]   As to Ockham's theory of motion Duhem says: "The affirmation that the continuation of
the local motion does not need any moving cause is
the law of inertia itself, formulated by Descartes; at
the time of Ockham it was too new to be admitted."[65]
With reference to Ockham's doctrine of action at
a distance we read the following statement: "By proclaiming the possibility of action at a distance, Ockham's theory prepares the modern doctrine of gravitation."[66]

Duhem's claims as to the place of the Parisian Nominalist School in the history of thought were embodied
in Überweg's monumental *Grundriss der Geschichte
der Philosophie* (Berlin, 1928). "The Parisian Ockhamist School," the text says, "turned out to be the
starting point of modern mechanics and astrophysics.
All the fundamental ideas which up until today used
to be attributed to Copernicus and Galileo, were here,
in the fourteenth century already, scientifically represented.[67]   The influence of this School on our modern
era is traced through the following Ockhamists: John
Buridan (died after 1358) rector of the University of
Paris, Nicholas of Oresme (d. 1382) Bishop of Lisieux,
Albert of Saxony (d. 1390) first rector of the University of Vienna, and Marsilius of Inghen (d. 1396) first
rector of the University of Heidelberg.   The name
of Nicholas of Oresme is pointed out with especial
emphasis.   This ingenious bishop besides being the
most outstanding national economist of the fourteenth
century outlined the doctrine of the daily rotation of

[64] P. Duhem, *Études sur Léonard de Vinci*, II, 86.
[65] Duhem, op. cit., II, p. 193.
[66] Duhem, op. cit., II, p. 86.
[67] Überweg, op. cit., II, p. 595.

the earth more precisely than Copernicus did.   In his
De difformitate qualitatum (1371), he discovered the
law of falling bodies generally connected with Galileo's
name.   In the same book he invented coordinate-
geometry two hundred and fifty years before Descartes,
thus assuring for his name the honor of being the in-
ventor of analytic geometry.

Concerning Buridan, Überweg makes the following
statement: "The impetus theory of Buridan and of his
school signifies a complete departure from Aristotelian
dynamics and astronomy and the beginning of the bril-
liant path of modern investigation of nature in Physics
and Astronomy.   It is not Copernicus and Galileo who
are to be considered as their founders but Buridan and
the Physicist School in Paris."[68]

The influence of these illustrious Parisian scientists
on Copernicus and Galileo can clearly be traced today.
Traces of Buridan's theory of impetus can be followed
in Cracow up to 1488, where Copernicus learned to
know it during his studies there in 1491.[69]   Buridan's
Physics found its way through Albert of Saxony to
Leonardo de Vinci[70] and to numerous Italian physicists
in the sixteenth century to be adopted later by Galileo,
the father of modern science and technique.

How far the philosophical personality of Ockham is
to be considered as the "spiritus rector" of these early
scientific movements only a more detailed research of
fourteenth-century manuscripts will establish.

[68] Überweg, op. cit., II, p. 598.   The French and German
translations from Duhem and Überweg are those of the author.

[69] Birkenmajer, in *Philosophisches Jahrbuch,* 35, 1922, 93;
in Überweg, op. cit., II, 598.

[70] Duhem, op. cit., II, 54-112.

OCKHAM'S ETHICAL PHILOSOPHY

W E HAVE BEEN examining in previous sections an extremely interesting combination of very different strains of thought in the philosophy of Ockham. A strange duality has been following us as we studied the epistemological aspects of Ockham's nominalism, which developed partly into a very definite type of empiricism, partly into a grammatico-logical schematism. The two emphases seemed to be quite divergent. The one resulted in a peculiarly emphatic intuitionalism with only concrete phenomena as its objects, the other in a highly abstract logical functionalism with nothing but signs as its objects.

Neither of the two motives of thought was found to have a very happy ending. Ockham's critical epistemology left a logic which was bound to develop into a mere science of signs and finally into a *scientia sermocinalis*. This feature became especially prominent in the case of the *suppositio simplex,* in which the terms of the propositions did not signify anything external, but stood only for their own concepts. The universals thus cut off from the external world became so etherealized that nothing else was left for the logician to do but to concentrate on the formal operations of the mind.[1] Critical epistemology, then, ended in formalism.

Critical empiricism traveled in an entirely different

[1] J. Maréchal, *Le Point de Depart de la Metaphisique,* (Bruges-Paris, 1923) 133 and 135: "La logique occamiste se resout tout entière en une logique de l'identité, en une Algebre de la Logique. Elle devient un jeu sterile de symboles, que les heritiers d'Occam vont compliquer de plus en plus et vider de contenu, au point de la ramener au niveau d'une grammaire."

direction. Our intuitions, deprived of the *species sensibiles,* were declared to be mental signs, mere representations of an external reality. Ockham declares that our intuitions, as entities distinct from their objects, may exist without their objects. We may see a star long after it has been destroyed. Again, God may cause in us the intuitive knowledge of a non-existent object. All these considerations point to the fact that our empirical data are only subjective representations which may not have anything behind them. Thus, critical empiricism ended in subjectivism.

The combined effect of this twofold criticism was naturally scepticism. The one emptied our abstract cognition and attenuated it into formal transparency. The other evaporated our intuitive cognition into possible will-o'-the-wisps. Both produced scepticism.

Scepticism is the mood of Ockhamist philosophy. It indicates a peculiar phase in the development of human reason. Reason after its separation from faith made a long journey. Its first sense of independence in the thirteenth century soon matured into criticism, (chiefly through Duns Scotus) and was followed shortly afterwards by its shadow, scepticism. The appearance of scepticism was due to the combination of two psychological factors: one was a keen realization of the inadequacy of reason's obtained results, the other an insufficient knowledge of reason's own nature. The awakening of the mind to the requirements of science which was far more advanced than the understanding of reason's limits and possibilities, resulted in a sense of disproportion, leaving a mental state of weakness, insufficiency and hopelessness behind. It was chiefly in Ockham's mind that all these motives reached their dramatic climax and became influential in stirring up an era of scepticism.

In attempting to present Ockham's ethical philosophy, a knowledge of his sceptical spirit is essential. All ethical theory is a relating of the human soul to some highest end. In the Middle Ages this end was identified with God, who was considered as the highest good.[2] Obviously, the kind of conception one had of God and of the soul exerted a tremendous influence on the formulation of one's ethics. Consequently, a study of how Ockham's scepticism shaped his conception of God and the soul, will be an instructive approach to his ethical philosophy.

Ockham's conception of God is a direct product of his nominalistic theory of knowledge. He differentiates a twofold knowledge, direct and indirect. We know directly when we know something in itself so that our intellect is determined by that thing alone, without the medium of any other thing distinguished from our object by reason or in reality. This direct knowledge may be intuitive or abstract, the latter meaning, of course, that type of knowledge which abstracts from the existence or non-existence of a thing. Another way of knowing is to know indirectly, that is, not in itself, but by the intermediacy of a certain concept which afterwards can be verified.

Applying these views to God, Ockham comes to the conclusion that because nothing can be known in itself, unless it is known intuitively,[3] God, Who cannot be known intuitively, cannot be known in Himself. Whatever we may know concerning God involves always the

[2] Aug., *Soliloquiorum libri,* II, Migne, P. L., 32-47, I, 2, n. 7 : "Deum et animam scire cupio. Nihilne plus ? Nihil omnino."

[3] *Sent.* I, dist. 3, qu. 2, E.

admixture of some intermediary concept which does not represent Him purely. In this conception the nominalistic havoc caused by Ockham's epistemological criticism may clearly be seen. Conceptual knowledge gives only approximations and conjectures; it never establishes real counterparts.

The analysis of the origin and formation of the concept "God" is highly original and in its empirical construction very significant. The divine essence is represented to us in a unique, composite concept the parts of which are abstracted naturally from external things. We may find many general traits common to God and to created things which can be abstracted. These several distinct traits coalesce in such a single concept as does not correspond to any other being. Thus, we form the concept of God and other things. God in this way is recognized in a composite concept which is absolutely unique in itself and cannot be verified in anything else, because by definition created wisdom is not created goodness and so on.

Ockham's analysis of the formation of this composite concept of God seems to neglect the formal principle which is operative in bringing together the various material traits of content; he is neglecting to explain why those traits "coalesce necessarily." There seems to be presupposed a certain *a priori* definition of what God *must* be according to which we construct His concept and in which the concept we produced is verified. This definition may vary in different individuals and ages. Its origin may be either arbitrary as that of the first principles of Hobbes,[4] or natural, in which case

4 Hobbes, *De Corpore,* cap. 25, 1: "Ratiocinationis prima principia, nempe definitiones, vera esse facimus nosmet ipsi per consensionem circa rerum appellationes."

the problem of innateness arises. Ockham's investigations leave both possibilities unanswered.

The concept of God does not necessarily involve the existence of God for Ockham. He rejects the Aristotelian arguments for the existence of a first mover. Aristotle's first point that whatever moves is moved by some other agent is not demonstrative, for we can reasonably say that the soul or an angel or even the weight which descends, moves itself. His second point that there cannot be in moving things a regress to infinity is eliminated by the necessity of assuming infinite process, as for instance in the case of a continuously long object which, if it is struck at a point, that is, at the end, moves the adjacent part, and that part moves the next, and so to infinity.[5]

Ockham's conclusions concerning the existence of a Deity are tainted with agnosticism although he accepts God as "presupposed by both philosophers and theologians."[6] He considers Aristotle's thesis relating to the existence of the unmoved mover more probable than its opposite but not as demonstrated. The same sceptical attitude is taken concerning the infinity of God: "Although God is efficient in everything, from this it does not follow that He is of infinite vigor. Effects which may be produced at once in an infinite number do not prove the infinity of the cause. Now, every effect which God may produce is finite, therefore, all effects together are finite also. Consequently, by their efficiency the infinity of God cannot be proved."[7]

[5] William of Ockham, *Centiloquium theologicum,* I, E. (Lúgdunii, 1495). This work is added to the voluminous Commentary to the *Sentences* of the 1495 edition.

[6] Ibid. I, A.

[7] *Quodlib.* 3, qu. 1: "Licet Deus sit efficiens omnium, tamen per hoc non potest probari, quod Deus sit infinitus in vigore,

What sort of an ethical theory can be expected with a conception of the highest Good as problematic as that of Ockham?

If we consider, now, the other pole of the traditional God-soul relationship, we are confronted again with the same spirit of scepticism. The rational soul, as a substance, participates in the inscrutable character of every substance. "A substance," according to his Commentary to the *Sentences,* "cannot be known by any composite concept proper to substances in such a manner that each of the partial concepts be abstracted from its subordinates. A substance is known only through connotative and negative concepts such as: an entity which subsists by itself; an entity not in another thing; an entity underlying all accidents, and so on."[8]   A further reason for our not being able to investigate substances is given by the fact that no substance acts except through its accidents."[9]   "When we see fire," so we are informed, "we know that it is fire; yet, in reality, we do not know fire in itself but only the accidents of fire."[10]   Accordingly, the soul as a substance cannot be known except through our mental states and facts of consciousness, and remains as to its inmost nature an unknowable domain.

It is no wonder that from such points of views the age-long tenets of rational psychology suffered a serious shake-up. Ockham became sceptical concerning the very existence of an immaterial and immortal soul and its essential functions. Aristotle's arguments did

quia effectibus infinitis simul producibilibus non potest probari infinitas causae; sed quilibet effectus ducibiles a Deo sunt finiti; ergo per efficientiam illorum non potest probari infinitas Dei."

[8] *Sent.* I, dist. 3, qu. 2, Y.

[9] Ibid. II, qu. 16, P.

[10] Ibid. I, dist. 3, qu. 2, E.

not disturb him much. The philosopher seems to have remained doubtful and undecided as to the real nature of the substantial form in man.

This conclusion discloses the deeply sceptical character of Ockham's notion of the soul. In his mind, the ancient foundation of the scholastic synthesis, stripped of its conceptual paraphernalia, became a shaky basis upon which to build an ethical theory in the traditional sense.

How, then, did Ockham succeed in formulating an ethical philosophy, that is, a study of the end of human conduct and of the principles whereby human acts must be regulated in order to attain to this end?

There was no way for him to find solid ground in the intellectual realm. The conceptual structures of the mind, undermined by his nominalism could not promise security. For him who could not find any proof for the existence of the soul, who rejected the Aristotelian formula of causal relation and thereby the stringency of the *a posteriori* proofs for the existence of God, the traditional bases of certainty crumbled away. On the other hand, he was not a mystically inclined soul. He could not find refuge from the sliding grounds of his scepticism in mystical union as many of his followers (Peter d'Ailly, John Gerson, Nicolaus Cusanus) tried to do. The way out for him was indicated by his temperament. He found security in ethical voluntarism, in the internally certain and evident experiences of a practical will.

The discovery of this road was prepared by his education in the Franciscan order. Unlike the Dominicans, who cultivated an intellectualistic theology to convince the heathen, the *fraticelli* of Saint Francis distinguished themselves by a practical piety devoted to converting the simple hearted and the poor. The practical character of the Franciscan Order led the *fratres minores* to adopt the voluntaristic and mystical outlook of Saint Augustine. The central principle of Augustinism is to be found in the principle of internality, the supposed key-word for all problems. It is in your internal experience that you have a certainty superior to any other certainty. The last word, the fulcrum of life is in you.[11] And it is not so much what you know as what you do that matters. *"Tanto sa, quanto fa"*—as Saint Francis of Assisi put it. For the content of your thought is only an expression of your inmost urge and action. Thus the Neo-Platonism of Plotinus in which the νοητòν, the known object, became absorbed by the νόησις, the knowing activity and experience,[12] found its continuation in the dynamic personality of Augustine.

The doctrine of the superiority of internal experiences can be traced clearly in Ockham's epistemology. In discussing the intellectual intuitions concerning our internal experiences, such as the acts of understanding, acts of will, pleasure, sorrow, he always attributes to them superiority over and above the sensuous, external experiences.

The retrenchment from the realm of sensuous experiences is the typical Augustinian attitude. It also became, as a matter of psychological need, the starting point of Ockham's ethical philosophy. Our external sensations possess merely a limited degree of certainty, not only because of their mere significatory character, but because one never knows whether or not God or

[11] Aug., *De Vera Religione*, Migne, P. L., 32-47, 39, 72: "Noli foras ire; in te ipsum redi; in interiore homine habitat veritas."
[12] Plotinus, *Enneads*, 5, 2, 2: "The nous *is* what it knows."

some other created agent is impressing a false picture
of the external world upon us.[13]   Certainty can be
secured only in our internal experiences, presented in
intellectual intuitions.

From such presuppositions it was quite natural to
arrive at the view of the preëminence of the will over
the other powers of the soul.   The will in Augustinian
psychology is considered as an absolute beginning
which by its elementary impulse directs the attention.
The attention fixed by the will produces clear and vivid
perceptions which in their intensity give a sense of
certainty.   From the awareness of the superiority of
internal certainty, therefore, the conclusion that the
will is the primary force in man, was quite inevitable.

Ockham accepted the will as the basis of his ethical
philosophy not only because of his Augustinian train-
ing, but because of his inborn disposition as well.
Ockham, the sharp, analytic thinker, the great scholar,
was basically a practical person. He took an active part
in life; in fact, the major part of his activities was not
scientific but polemic and bellicose.   His life was not
spent in the silence of a cell, but in the fight of the
Spirituals of his order for evangelical poverty, in travels, in the prison of the pope at Avignon (1324-1328),
in the adventures of escape (end of May, 1328), in
excommunication (June 6, 1328), in the field-camp of
Louis of Bavaria in Pisa, in the imperial court of Munich (after 1330), at the Diets of the Empire (in
1338), and in delivering a veritable shower of political
writings against the pope.   His life spent in revolt and
fight, found a tragic end in the black plague which

[13] Read *Quodlib.* V, qu. 5 in McKeon's translation (*Selections from Medieval Philosophers,* vol. II. p. 371), where we
are instructed that the sight of a thing may remain by the
power of God when that thing is non-existent.

devastated Europe in 1349. It was to be expected that a turbulent personality such as that of the Invincible Doctor was to interpret human conduct in terms of will.

Ockham's philosophy of will is based on the foundation of the real unity of all mental phenomena, a view which he inherited from the deep insight of Augustine. The difference between intellect and will is purely logical and it indicates only the various manners in which the substance of the soul can act. In what sense, then, does Ockham attribute superiority to the will as against the intellect? His own words explain this in the following manner: "the will may be called superior to the intellect, because the act of loving, designated by the word will, is superior to the act of understanding, designated by the word intellect."[14]

The real significance of the primacy of will is psychological and epistemological. Ockham follows here the greatest psychologist of the Middle Ages, Augustine, and also Duns Scotus, whose views on this point are the same. For the Bishop of Hippo, the entire process of knowing, from the fact of awareness to the acts of judging and reasoning, is conditioned and formed completely under the purposive impulses of the will.[15] Ockham takes the same position. He argues for the complete passivity of the intellect in the name of his law of parsimony.

In the case of necessary propositions the assent is caused by the knowledge of the terms without any act of the intellect of its own; in other cases, however, the immediate cause of both sensitive and intellectual cognition is volition. Ockham points out with keen psychological sense that "the grade of intensity, of the

[14] *Sent.* II, qu. 24, P.

[15] Aug., *De Trinitate,* Migne, P. L., 32-47, Book XI.

conatus and attention in our cognition cannot be caused at all without the act of the will."[16] The truly important point, however, is his epistemological remark concerning the relation of will and intellect: "I say that the cause, as a result of which a true rather than a false proposition is formed, an affirmative rather than a negative, is the will, because the will wants to form the one and not the other."[17]

The significance of this thought is tremendous. It connects Ockham's logic and epistemology and his entire empirical ideation with the will and his ethics. Without this sentence, or its equivalent, the above mentioned parts of his philosophy would only be artificially added to his ethics without any organic interrelation. A study of the psychological and epistemological influence of the will on the cognitive process reveals the deep undertow which carries the whole current of his philosophy. This deep undertow comes to its original expression in Ockham's ethics where an insistent voluntarism is the dominant tone. From here it is naturally expanded to all the rest of the parts, permeating and combining the whole into an organic system.

In the light of the central significance of Ockham's philosophy of will, his ethics is quite simplified. The Augustinian principle of the all-pervasiveness of the will[18] is for him, too, the fundamental principle. Consequently, the problem of ethics is synonymous with the problem of will.

The human will according to its nature is related to some ultimate end. This end is normative for the for-

[16] *Sent.* II, qu. 26, U.

[17] *Sent.* II, qu. 25, K.

[18] Aug., *De civ. Dei*, XIV, 6. "Voluntas est quippe in omnibus, immo omnes nihil quam voluntates sunt."

mation of conduct and is decisive for the moral quality of our actions. To the question what constitutes the ultimate end of man Ockham answers that the ultimate end may be considered objectively, as the source of our happiness, or subjectively, as the actual enjoyment of the feeling of happiness, the seat of which for Ockham as for Duns Scotus is the will. Loving, not contemplating, constitutes the essence of happiness.

The human will confronted with its ultimate end may either move toward it or may turn away from it. In the first case we are led by love, in the second by hatred or detestation. Ockham's fundamental view concerning this situation is that the will is not necessarily attracted by the ultimate end. To establish his thesis he had to direct his arguments against the Thomistic view of his age which, guided by an intellectual determinism, adopted just the opposite of his belief. According to Thomas Aquinas the objective end of man is God; the formal end consists in the consecution or possession of this objective end which is the essence of human happiness.[19] By possessing God man realizes his highest perfection. Moreover, every being is perfect, insofar as it is in act and operation. It is necessary, then, that the supreme perfection of man should consist in the highest actuality of man. We attain this perfection in that activity of our intellect whereby God is presented to us. Therefore, the height of our perfection and, consequently, of our happiness consists in the act of intellect.[20]

Concerning this ultimate end, Thomas Aquinas taught that man's appetite is filled with it so completely

[19] *Summa Theol.*, (London: Burns, Oates, and Washbourne, 1920), I-IIae, qu. 1, art. 8.

[20] *Summa Theol.*, I-IIae, qu. 3, art. 2 and 4.

that nothing else is left to be desired.[21] In his view, everything seeks its own perfection by natural compulsion, and nothing is free from this universal necessitation. Man is determined intrinsically to seek his own perfection and happiness. This inner compulsion, however, does not take away his freedom because by that compulsion man is necessitated according to the inclination of his nature. Only then is something compelled and consequently not free, when it is coerced to do or suffer something against its natural inclination. Freedom and intrinsic natural compulsion are not contradictory. In the words of the Angelic Doctor, "to be moved from within, that is, by an intrinsic principle, is to be moved voluntarily."[22] Our freedom consists only in the selection of one rather than other means along the way toward the irresistible end.

This principle of deterministic ethics was carried to its limit by Ockham's contemporary, Thomas Bradwardine, (1290-1349), Archbishop of Canterbury, who developed it into a complete theological determinism. God is absolutely sovereign and nothing can resist Him. His will is all-victorious, predetermining things to conservation or perdition, perfection or destruction, glory or misery. The freedom which the "doctor profundus" leaves for man is nothing but an "unperceived necessitation." Only *perceived* necessitation would mean lack of freedom and coercion. In the words of his chief work (*De Causa Dei adversus Pelagium*): "Although somebody is compelled to do something, good or bad, if he does not know this necessity and acts voluntarily and freely as far as it is in his power, the

[21] *Summa Theol.*, I-IIae, qu. 1, art. 5.

[22] *Summa Theol.*, I, qu. 105, art. 4 and 2.

resulting act will be meritorious."[23] This ruthless type of determinism, representing the infiltration of the "Islam" or "Submission" theology of the Arabs (Averroes, Avicenna, Avempace, and especially Algazel) into the West, became the source of the Calvinistic-predestinational world-view through the theology of Wyclif (d. 1384) who was deeply influenced by it.

Against the invasion of this oriental submissive and passive theology, William of Ockham once more revived the active, Indo-European spirit of his fellow countryman, Pelagius, the Briton (ca. 420), by proclaiming full freedom for the human will. Ockham's definition of freedom is this: "I call freedom a power whereby I can bring forth an effect indifferently and contingently so that I can produce the same effect and not produce it without undergoing any change in that power."[24] Against the assumption that man is compelled to seek his ultimate end, that is, perfection and happiness, he argues in this manner: "It is to be denied that everything by nature's necessity has an inclination, in the strict sense of the word, toward its own perfection. This is true only if the thing to be perfected is active by natural necessity, which cannot be said about the will."[25]

Ockham insists on the indeterminate character of will both in relation to the ultimate end and in the choice

[23] Thomas Bradwardine, *De Causa Dei,* III, cap. 1, cor. p. 644 B, in Dr. Sebastian Hahn, *BGPM,* vol. V, heft. 2: "Ex his autem evidenter apparet, quod licet quis necessitatus fuerit ad faciendum quicquam boni vel mali, si tamen necessitationem illam ignoret et faciat hoc voluntarie et libere, quantum in se est, meretur."

[24] *Quodlib.* I, u. 16: "Voco libertatem potestatem, qua possum indifferenter et contingenter effectum ponere, ita quod possum eundem effectum causare et non causare, nulla diversitate circa illam potentiam facta."

[25] *Sent.* I, dist. 2, qu. 1, X.

of means leading to that end. Man is free; he may
desire happiness or he may not. Ockham alludes to
instances which show that believers in a future life
kill themselves with the full use of their reason just as
unbelievers do. Again, if the ultimate end would coerce us efficiently we would be necessitated to choose
the means, too, that are indispensable for the end. Yet,
we see that some of the faithful who are fully convinced that happiness cannot be attained without a good
life, do not care to lead a good life. Therefore, the
will is free both in intending the means that promote an
end, as well as in intending an end. To be sure, the
will is embedded in the mechanism of natural impulses
and habits which may thwart the free determination
of man. Ockham is sensitive to the mechanistic character of natural volition and adds that in an act, caused
by a habit, the will is not free.

The idea of a natural impulse or habit, antecedent
in the will, brings us to the problem of causation with
reference to human action. What, in the last analysis,
is the genesis of our actions? The knowledge of end
and means is an inducement to act, yet we have found
that the will is not necessitated by any intellectual motive and is free in choosing any possible course. What,
then, moves the will, when the will refuses to be influenced by intellectual presentations? Is the will an absolute, unmotivated start or is it subject to some metaphysical causation? Considerations of this sort had
been basically important for medieval moral philosophy, and Ockham could not evade facing them.

Ockham's answers to these questions are particularly
interesting because of their connection with the law of
causality in general. The question whether the human
will is a cause or not cannot be settled because "we

cannot demonstrate whether something is a cause or not."[26]   This is a typically Humeian sentence, expressing Ockham's scepticism concerning the possibility of establishing the causal relation.   The examples which he uses leave no doubt as to the proper meaning of his startling utterance: "Although burning always follows the contact of fire with an inflammable object, this does not exclude the possibility that its cause is not the fire.   It may be that God has so ordained things that whenever fire is compresent with the object, He Himself is the cause of burning."[27]   This comparison is an ancient one.   It was used as early as in the eleventh century by the sceptic Arab Algazel (1059-1111), who in his *Tahafut al-Falasifa* (the destruction of philosophers), expressed his doubts as to the necessary connection between cause and effect.[28]   The strange thing is that Algazel's thesis, which was ridiculed by the scholastics as extreme, found a late friend in the person of Ockham, although no connection can be established between the two thinkers.[29]   Ockham goes even so far as actually to doubt the possibility of proving whether anyone is a human being or not.

[26] *Sent.* II, qu. 5, R. S.

[27] Ibid.

[28] In Stöckl, *Geschichte der Philosophie des Mittelalters* (Mainz, 1865) II, 206-207: *Destructio destructionis,* disp. 1, in physicis dub. 3, ad. Venet. 1527: "Quaero quae est ratio, quod ipse sit agens?   Et non habent (philosophi) rationem, nisi testimonium adventus combustionis cum tactu ignis.   Sed testimonium indicat, quod advenit cum eo, et non indicat, quod advenit ex eo, et quod non sit causa alia praeter eum."

[29] Robert Grosseteste, first Chancellor of the University of Oxford in 1253 left all his books to Adam Marsh and the Franciscan convent at Oxford (Cf. Little, op. cit., p. 57). Grosseteste quotes, in his books, the Arabs, Avicenna, Averroes, Albumasar and was very familiar with the aristotelian-arabian literature.   Ockham might have had, therefore, in the convent, contact with the Arabs.

To explain the genesis of human volition and free choice, Ockham assumes the immediate causality of God, although he does not claim demonstrability for this hypothesis.[30] He defines an immediate cause as a phenomenon in the presence of which the effect follows and in the absence of which the effect does not follow. Ockham, however, is not an occasionalist who considers God as immediately or mediately the only causal principle. He strongly emphasizes the human will as an immediate, although secondary cause. In Ockham's view, although man always acts with God, Who is a co-agent concurring with him as a primary cause, nevertheless, the will, when all is told, is a genuine initiator, and man is exclusively responsible for his deeds. This is the Scotist doctrine of indeterminism which rejects a predestination of man *ante praevisa merita*. Ockham, by eliminating the total causality of God in the will, discarded *eo ipso* any antecedent predestination also. Contrarily, in his belief, man is the maker of his own destiny.

Ockham's philosophy of will, expressed in terms of pure and spontaneous beginnings, saves the dignity of man, and was to bear fruit later in the individualism of the Renaissance, but does it save the dignity and absolute sovereignty of God? This question placed Ockham before the *crux theologorum* of all times. The position he took is typical of his mentality. The answer he gives is that of the sceptic and agnostic: *ignoramus et ignorabimus*. Although he likes to develop speculations on the basis of assumptions, when he is urged for demonstrative reasons he confesses that nobody is able to find out whether the decisions of God are actualized by Him alone or with the cooperation of

[30] *Sent.* I, dist. 25, qu. unica G.

created agents. It is impossible to know whether God is the total cause of anything or not. For that reason it cannot be decided whether God's will always prevails or is at times foiled. Concerning this problem reason's only course is to refrain from judgment.

Having declined to enter the theological discussion of the nature of predestination, Ockham continues to investigate the principles which determine the conduct of man to attain his end. The will is free in its decision to choose the means which bring man forward toward the goal. Freedom alone, however, may mean only haphazard action without any guarantee as to its results, unless morality is placed on deeper and more secure foundations. The chief aim of every ethical philosophy is to give a norm of morality and point out the ultimate principles which are to regulate the activity of will. What is the normative principle of the will in Ockham's ethics?

In describing the operation of will Ockham assumed the continuous concurrence of the will of God. This close and essential parallelism between the primary and secondary cause led him naturally to seek for the foundations of the moral will in the very will of God.

Where else could he have looked for the ultimate basis of morality? For all those who accepted the ideology of Plato in its Augustinian and Thomistic interpretation, that is, as universal ideas in the mind of God (*universalia ante rem*), the basis of all existence was constituted by the intellectual essence of God. The essence of God is identical with the ideas of God, and the imitability of these ideas is the source of all truth, goodness, and beauty in the created world. Ockham did not accept universal ideas in God as *a priori* archetypes of the world. For him whatever God knows is individual and the universal is known by Him only in so far as He sees acts of intellect in our soul as signs for many things. Yet the ideas in God are not *a posteriori* representations of things already created. The ideas of God are independent of the created world and are creations of His intellect. That is, the ideas in God according to Ockham are not antecedent to His thinking but are produced by and in the very act of thinking. Ockham's conception of the divine intellect is rooted in act and creation, that is, in volition. Consequently, to find the foundations of morality he had to recur to the will of God as constituting the essence of God.

The ground of all moral goodness or evil was discovered by Ockham in the free will of God. The first question which here arises is how Ockham established freedom in the will which is the source of everything. It must be noted that Ockham never claimed a demonstrative proof for the freedom of human will; therefore, *a fortiori,* he cannot be expected to have such a proof for the divine will. Concerning the freedom of man's will he says: "The freedom of will cannot be proved by any reason, for all reason which is produced as demonstrative, adopts things that are just as doubtful, and just as unknown, to lead to a conclusion or more unknown. Yet we may know it evidently by experience, by being aware that no matter how reason dictates something, the will can accept it or reject it."[31] He expresses himself in the same manner with regard

[31] *Quodlib.,* I, qu. 16: "Non potest probari (libertas voluntatis) per aliquam rationem, quia omnis ratio probans accipit aeque dubia et aeque ignotum conclusioni vel ignotius. Potest tamen evidenter cognosci per experientiam, per hoc, quod homo experitur, quod quantumcumque ratio dictet aliquid, potest tamen voluntas hoc velle vel nolle."

to the will of God, and says that it is a matter of belief only that God is a free cause. The argument with
which he recommends his thesis is that of the *analogia
hominis*.[32] As in the case of man, so with reference to
God, no other reason can be given why among many
possibilities one is actualized rather than the rest, except the free choice of the agent. In the last analysis
the establishment of the freedom of God is an extension of the irreducible inner experience of man, whereby we feel that in our inmost being we are free.

The idea of a free Deity is of tremendous influence
on the moral order. If God is absolutely free He may
change the present moral order or even the laws of
nature and give another world-order of an entirely
different character. Ockham does not hesitate to draw
this conclusion: "God cannot be obligated to any
act."[33] To be sure, Ockham is not the first thinker to
come to this result. Duns Scotus, with whom Ockham
shares so many views, expressed the same idea before
him when he said: "There is no other reason why the
will intended something, save that the will is will . . .
since there is no prior cause."[34] Again, Ockham's famous contemporary Thomas Bradwardine used the
very same language, saying that "precisely because
God intends the occurrence of something in a certain
way, it is reasonable that it happen in this way, not

[32] Quodlib., I, qu. 16: "Every cause which cannot be impeded
may face everything, in fact, even infinity itself, indifferently.
If at a given moment it actualizes one of the many possibilities,
no other reason than its being a free agent can be given for its
producing one effect rather than another. But God is such a
cause with respect to all things produced by Him from eternity.
Therefore, it is to be accepted as a fact that God is a cause
which acts contingently."

[33] *Sent.* II, qu. 9, F.

[34] Duns Scotus, *Opus Oxoniense,* I, d. 8, qu. 5, n. 24. Quoted
in Überweg, op. cit., II, p. 516.

contrarily."[35]   Is, then, Ockham only reaffirming the views of these voluntarists?

The great difference between the view of Scotus and Bradwardine on one side and that of the Venerabilis Inceptor on the other side is due to the nominalism of the latter.   Both Scotus and Bradwardine build, in the last analysis, on the intellectual essence of God, that is, on the blueprint of a *lex aeterna,* which furnishes the antecedent motives for divine action.   The will of God is indeterminate, yet can never do anything contradictory to His own essence.   For Scotus, God can never change the first two commandments of the decalogue without overthrowing the laws of logic which bind even His will.

Ockham's Deity is not bound by any intellectual essence or eternal ideas constituting this essence, neither is He tied by the laws of logic or nature.   His will is absolutely creative.   Just as his ideas are brought forth as sparks of a creative action, His decisions and deeds are the products of a purely aboriginal volitional nisus.

As a result of these views, Ockham, leaving the cautious language of Scotus,[36] arrived at the following revolutionary conclusions: "God cannot be obligated to any act.   With him a thing becomes right solely for

[35] Thomas Bradwardine, *De Causa Dei,* I, cap. 21, p. 231, in Dr. Sebastian Hahn, "Thomas Bradwardinus und seine Lehre von der menschlichen Willensfreiheit," *BGPM,* Vol. V, heft. 2: "Imo quia Deus vult sic fieri, rationabilis est, quod sic fiat, non e contra."

[36] Duns Scotus, *Op. Ox.* IV, d. 46, qu. 1, n. 6: "Sed non potest (Deus) aliquid velle, quod non possit recte velle, quia voluntas sua est prima regula."   Quoted in Überweg, op. cit. II. p. 516.   *Op. Ox.* I, d. 44, qu. un. n. 2: "Ideo sicut potest aliter agere, ita potest aliam legem statuere rectam, quia si statueretur a Deo, recta esset, quia nulla lex est recta, nisi quatenus a voluntate divina acceptatur."

the reason that He wants it to be so."[37]   Sinful acts
are sins only according to our present moral order.
Absolutely considered, however, acts such as adultery,
stealing, and the like, if performed by God or if after
divine institution are performed by man, would become
virtues. God could pronounce the hatred of his name
a righteous act just as well as He now does the opposite. Sin does not exist except in an act of will when
man neglects an obligation or does something contrary
to an obligation. Since, however, our obligations depend upon the *potentia ordinaria* of God, they have no
absolute binding significance. God with His *potentia
absoluta* may obligate us differently. Therefore, our
sins might become virtues, and vice versa, if God in His
absolute freedom would introduce a different moral
order.

These doctrines whose effect was characterized by
the report of the masters of theology in Paris in 1326
as "pestilential," introduced an entirely new element
into ethics, namely, that of moral relativism. There
seemed to be no absolute norm of morality left either
in man or in God. "Recta ratio," "natural law," "eternal law," the ancient rocks of moral security lost their
absolute character with the disappearance of an absolute norm in the essence of God. With the conception
of a Deity, Who is essentially unguarded in His intrinsic nature, incalculable and unpredictable, nothing
seemed to be eternally and inalienably permanent. The
idea of an unconditionally free God brought in its
wake the idea of relativity.

Thoughts like these make and mark history. The
obedient, humble spirit of the churchly Middle Ages
expressed by Thomas Aquinas in such words as that

[37] *Sent.* II, qu. 9, F.

"moral goodness has necessarily to depend upon the eternal law rather than upon reason,"[38] suffered a serious set-back. Conscience, that is, the dictate of reason, was left by itself as a life-boat tossed on heavy sea-waters. For how should man now know the moral law? He might, for the time rely on the actual moral order of the *potestas ordinaria,* yet how can he be assured against a slow or abrupt invasion of the *potestas absoluta* in the temporary arrangement of the present? What are the criteria of valid morality in the changing moments of history?

To affirm that one should consult the will of God would amount to a mockery rather than to an answer. "Who ever entered the secrets of God and who was His consiliary?" One might conceivably wait for a revelation of the will of God in prophets and saints, popes and church gatherings. In this case, however, the result would not be knowledge but faith and blind acceptance. The last and only possible solution is to investigate the creative will of God in so far as it is immanent in the course of nature, in the developments of history, and in the silent gropings of our own heart. With the acceptance of this arduous task modern history begins.

[38] *Summa Theol.,* I-IIae, qu. 19, art. 4: "Necessarium est bonitatem magis ex lege aeterna quam ex ratione dependere."

OCKHAM'S POLITICAL PHILOSOPHY

WILLIAM OCKHAM'S INTERESTS were
turned to political philosophy by the circumstances of his life. As early as 1323, he became en-
tangled in the controversy of his order on evangelical
poverty with the pope, John XXII, who by his bull,
Ad conditorem canonum, issued on December 8, 1322,
withdrew from the Franciscans the right of holding
property in the name of the Holy See, granted to them
by Innocent IV in 1245, and by Nicholas III in 1279.
The case seems trifling, yet it involved the interpretation of the life of Christ himself, whom the sons of St.
Francis tried to imitate by substituting the use of property for its ownership. The "Spirituals" stood for the
original views of the order and considered the papal
bull as dragging them down to worldliness and abase-
ment. Ockham in a sermon delivered at Bologna at-
tacked the pope's conception of apostolic poverty. John
XXII, in a bull dated December 1, 1323, addressed to
the bishops of Ferrara and Bologna, ordered his ar-
rest and held him in Avignon four years for trial.
In August, 1325, a commission of six theologians, one
of whom was Durandus de St. Porciano, at that time
Bishop of Meaux, was appointed to investigate his
theological and philosophical doctrines. In 1326 the
commission declared fifty-one articles taken from his
Commentary to the *Sentences* as heretical. On April
13, 1328, Ockham signed the protest of the general of
the Franciscan order, Michael Cesena, also under ar-
rest, against the papal bull of 1322, which condemned
the tenet of evangelical poverty. The night of May

24, 1328, brought a dramatic turn in his life. He succeeded in escaping from the papal prison in the company of Cesena and Bonagratia of Bergamo, the famous civil and canon lawyer, and fled to Pisa to seek the protection of Louis of Bavaria, emperor of Germany and arch-enemy of the pope. John XXII sent bull after bull to have the trio arrested, but they found a safe haven in Munich under the protection of the emperor. There Ockham met with Marsiglio of Padua (d. 1342 or 1343) and John of Jandun (d. 1328), also fugitives from the pope. Ockham's excommunication followed on June 6, 1328. He lived thenceforth in the Franciscan convent at Munich, attended the diets of Rhense and Frankfurt in 1338, and stood by the emperor to the latter's death in 1347.

According to a chronicler who wrote about 1349, Ockham offered his pen to the emperor in exchange for the protection of his sword in the well-known words: *"tu me defendas gladio, ego te defendam calamo."* He kept his promise by issuing a long array of polemical writings against the pope and the misdemeanors of the church at Avignon. The first of these writings was his *Opus nonaginta dierum,* in 1330 or 1332; this was followed by the *Tractatus de dogmatibus Johannis XXII Papae,* in 1333 or 1334; *Epistola ad Fratres Minores in capitulo apud Assisium congregatos,* in 1334; *Opusculum adversus errores Johannis XXII,* in 1335; *Compendium errorum Johannis XXII Papae,* between 1335 and 1338; *Defensorium contra Johannem XXII,** between 1335 and 1349; *Tractatus ostendens quod Benedictus Papa XII nonnullas Johannis XXII haereses amplexus est et defendit,* about 1338; *Dia-*

---

* This book according to I. Müller, (*Zeitschrift für Kirchengeschichte,* VI, 78-82) can no longer be ascribed to Ockham.

logus inter Magistrum et Discipulum de Imperatorum et Pontificum potestate, between 1334 (first part) and 1336 to 1339 (third part) ; *Tractatus de potestate imperiali,* after 1339 ; *Octo questiones super potestate ac dignitate papali,* between 1339 and 1342 ; *De Imperatorum et Pontificum potestate,* in 1346 or 1347 ; *De electione Caroli IV,* at the beginning of 1348.

The works which most extensively represent Ockham's doctrines of political philosophy are the *Eight Questions concerning the Power and Dignity of the Pope,* and especially the long treatise of the *Dialogue between Master and Disciple on the Power of Emperors and Popes.* The form of both works is academic, presenting views *pro* and *con* without decision. In the prologue of the *Dialogue* the disciple particularly asks the master not to express his own views for fear that he might be influenced by them. For that reason it is not an easy task to form from these works a clear idea of Ockham's personal views.

The general motive of Ockham's political writings is to bring about a betterment in the affairs of the church. The sad plight of Catholic Christianity during the stay of the papal court at Avignon gave ample material for his crusading. He does not write as a scholar and dispassionate theoretician but as a polemicist and propagandist. While discussing matters of the Holy Roman Empire and the power of the emperor, he keeps the church constantly before his mind as his chief concern. His pledge to defend Louis IV with his pen led him to promote the cause of the church rather than to plead the cause of the emperor. He writes not as a courtier to advocate the case of a crown, be it right or wrong,[1] but as a prophet whose voice in the wilderness prepares the way for a better day.

Keeping this point before our minds we shall not find it disappointing that Ockham's political philosophy is not presented in a systematic way, but is incidentally scattered among his ecclesiastico-political writings and is auxiliary to his primary concern. It would be in vain to search for a theory of state as such. Nevertheless, subordinated to his main motive we find many remarkable views on political philosophy which were powerful enough to attract the attention not only of his age but of the following centuries as well.

In Ockham's view the original state of man was a state of nature directed by the laws of nature as revealed by natural reason. "All men were created equal as to what concerns the sustentation of the body, the procreation of children, the contracting of matrimony or observing virginity, and such others.[2] In this state of nature, he says "man is not obliged to obey man but God alone,"[3] and all property is in common. Man, however, lost this state of original vigor, and it was found necessary to build the state by a "general com-

[1] Because of his moderate and impartial attitude in the conflict between emperor and pope he was called later by Thomasius, in his *Historia contentionis inter Imperium et Sacerdotium* (1722), p. 107, "adulator, homo ambidexter, neutralista, timidus . . . pessimum genus hominum ad maximas turbas in Republica excitandas," etc. Cf. James Sullivan, "Marsiglio of Padua and William of Ockham," *American Historical Review,* II (1897), p. 606.

[2] *Dialogus,* in M. Goldast's *Monarchia,* (Frankfurt, 1614), II, 893, 1.3: "Omnes homines natura sunt pares: puta in his, quae pertinent ad corporis sustentationem et prolis generationem, sicut de matrimonio contrahendo, vel virginitate servanda, vel aliquo huiusmodi."

All quotations in this article are original translations of the author.

[3] Ibid.: "Homo homini obedire non tenetur, sed soli Deo."

pact of human society.[4] The members of this society surrendered part of their rights to a chosen prince who was elected to rule. The aim of society is the cultivation of the common good safeguarded by civil laws. The right of owning private property was established and secured by law. Legislation is vested in each member of the community, for "that which touches all must be acted on by all."[5] The right of making laws, however, can be delegated to a chosen body or to the prince. The supreme power of the prince is limited by the law of nature and by the positive law common to all nations. If the executive power oversteps the limits of his power, the people may use sword against him. This theory of the right of revolution without any qualification as to private judgment presents a strong evaluation of the human personality as against the corporate political body, reflecting Ockham's emphasis on the concrete and individual in his theory of knowledge as against the general and universal.

The outstanding feature of Ockham's political philosophy must be sought in his energetic reduction of all political and social phenomena to the laws of nature. In the midst of his over-abundant quotations from the Scriptures we see him seeking for the ultimate principles in the laws of nature as manifested in the will of the individual seeking his own good. This feature is intimately connected with Ockham's emphasis on the all-controlling position of the common good (*utilitas communis*) in which all private interests are united. Laws are made for the sake of general welfare. If the common good requires it, private property may be

[4] *Dialogus,* in M. Goldast's *Monarchia,* (Frankfurt, 1614) II, p. 924m, 1.60: "Generale pactum societatis humanae."

[5] Ibid., p. 934, 1.15: "Quod omnes tangit debet tractari per omnes."

abolished. The reason for collecting taxes can be only the common good. The prince has not to conform to the *jus gentium* if it is injurious to the common good. Another conception which points out clearly Ockham's insistence on the normative force of nature is his theory of sovereignty or plenary power (*plenitudo potestatis*) as residing in the ruler. He defines sovereignty as the power by virtue of which the ruler can do anything that is not expressly contrary to the law of God and of nature.[6] Sovereignty, then, is limited in its practice by that which is ultimately normative in all manifestations of the life of a state: the laws of nature and God.

Ockham's doctrines, however, are not exhausted by a theoretical indication of the ultimate principle which has to regulate all political life, but they include practical directions as well concerning the technique of asserting this principle. Nature's laws as immanent in the primitive instincts of the will are to be recognized and brought to prominence in certain channels in order to utilize their guiding function toward the common good. Ockham developed these practical instructions in his doctrine of representation.

The idea of representation was theoretically accepted in the Roman point of view that the emperor was the representative of the people, and in the fiction that the electoral princes of Germany represented the people of the whole world. Ideas such as these found their practical application to the times by the powerful pen of Marsiglio of Padua, Ockham's famous contemporary. His monumental work, *The Defender of Peace*

[6] W. A. Dunning, *A History of Political Theories* (New York, 1902) I, 249: ". . . ut omnia possit quae non sunt expresse contra legem Dei neque ius naturae."

(*Defensor Pacis*), published in 1324, announced for the first time that "according to the truth and the opinion of Aristotle, . . . the legislative power is reserved to the totality of the people or a majority of them through their election or will, expressed orally in a general assembly of the people."[7]   This thesis is the first clear and outspoken formulation of the sovereignty of the people as the source of all political power, and as such is of enormous significance for the modern history of political theories.   Ockham, although not the first to announce the same view, expressed it just as definitely and originally.   Marsiglio and Ockham, writing almost at the same time, were independent of each other.   According to the accurate and exhaustive discussion of James Sullivan, "so entirely opposed are the theories of the two men, so totally different are their conceptions of the church and the state that it is difficult to see on what grounds Clement VI accused Marsiglio of borrowing from Ockham."[8]   The differences between the two men are explained with fine understanding by Kenneth Brampton in the following words:

> With the characteristic mentality of his race Ockham accepted the world as he found it, and was prepared with patience to turn all things to the best advantage. Far different from this conservative attitude is the radicalism of Marsilius, to whose mind—fired with Latin enthusiasm—the world as it ought to be stood out in bold relief from the world as it really is. Such an author will

[7] *Defensor Pacis* I, 12, in Goldast's *Monarchia*, II, 169: ". . . civium universalitatem aut eius valentiorem partem per suam electionem seu voluntatem in generali civium congregatione per sermonem expressam . . ."

[8] Speech of July 11, 1343: "Hoc dicimus propter illum Guillelmum Occam qui diversos errores contra potestatem et auctoritatem sancte sedis docuit et docet, et ab illo Guillelmo didicit et recepit errores ille Marsilius et multi alii" (Ibid. p. 416).

tend to display clarity of vision, impatience of expression, and completeness of conception; and he will impress us with the feeling that his brilliance, crystallized into a single volume, leaves but little room for development. But Ockham grows from volume to volume, and travels much farther for not knowing at first how far he intended to go. His painful efforts to fix his beliefs obscure his style but illumine his methods; and the principles unravelled in this process are all the more forceful for being based on reluctant conviction.[9]

Ockham's theory of representation may be summed up in this manner. The election of the prince and the legislation belong to every member of society. In appointing the prince, the people invest him with their own rights,[10] yet retain as much liberty as considerations of the common good may permit.[11] He is particularly anxious to retain freedom of speech.

Ockham is apparently against capital punishment, for he teaches that nobody should be deprived of his life.[12] What the sovereign people is to the state, the general council is to the church. The church is not the pope and the clergy, but the collective body of the faithful who believe in Christ. Power, therefore, comes not from above but from below, from the representatives of the people, including laity, both men and women.[13] In his meticulous manner Ockham describes in detail the plan of a general council which is entirely original with him. His project, outlined in

[9] K. C. Brampton, *The De Imperatorum and Pontificum Potestate of William of Ockham,* (Oxford: Clarendon Press, 1927), p. xxvii.

[10] *Dialogus,* p. 923, 11, 25ff.

[11] Ibid., p. 924, 1.60 and *Octo Quaest.,* p. 386, 11.5ff.

[12] Ibid., p. 932, 1.64.

[13] Ibid., pp. 604, 605. Marsiglio excluded women.

the *Dialogus,* is summed up by Dunning in the following manner:

> Assuming the right of every people, every com-
> munity, and every corporation (*corpus*) to legis-
> late under certain circumstances for itself . . . he
> (Ockham) points out that the legislative body
> could be constituted as follows: a primary assem-
> bly of all believers in each parish or other small
> community could choose delegates to an electoral
> assembly for the diocese or kingdom or other po-
> litical division, and by these assemblies the dele-
> gates to the council could be chosen; and such a
> council would truly represent the church, even
> though there should be no Pope to summon or to
> preside over it.[14]

Ockham's and Marsiglio's democratic conception of
representation were not only influential in paving the
road for the great pre-Reformation councils held at
Constance in 1414-1418 and at Basel in 1431-1443, but
also in preparing the day of a democratic state built on
the consent of the governed.

The problem of the relationship of church and state
thus built up on the representation of the people found
a different treatment by Marsiglio and Ockham. While
for Marsiglio the highest institution on earth is the
state, (priests, bishops and pope constituting only one
class among the many working for the common good),
Ockham adopts the theory of Dante both with refer-
ences to the universal monarchy and the parallel standing of state and church. Emperor and pope are each
supreme in their own domain. Nevertheless, pope and
emperor may occasionally interfere with each other.
The pope and any other ecclesiastic may be tried before
a secular court in temporal crimes. If the pope and
clergy resist, arms may be used against them. Ockham

14 Dunning, op. cit., I, 252.

is especially emphatic in rejecting the papal claim of confirming the Roman emperor in his office.

In the election of the emperor, according to Ockham, the pope's only part is anointing and crowning him. If the emperor is unjust in performing his duties in temporal matters, the pope may enforce his deposition by spiritual, not by forcible means.

Ockham's political writings were motivated chiefly by zeal for the church and by an ardent desire to improve her demoralized condition, the cause of which he found in the arrogance and usurpation of the popes. He is remarkably fair. Without any trace of animosity he seems to be led exclusively by sincere intention to help both the pope and the faithful and to be instrumental in bringing about peace.

Characteristic is Ockham's constant appeal to the Scriptures as the final source of authority, an appeal in which we notice the distant voice of the Reformation.

Ockham's main intention in his anti-papal writings is to define in all precision the limits of the papal power as a guarantee of peaceful and promising church-life. He is convinced that order and smooth operation require authority in the church. An exact specification of this jurisdiction will bring peace; neglect of it discord and revolt.

It may be regretted that Ockham the philosopher spent the last two decades (1328-1349) of his all too short life in the relentless struggle of his age between the rising national consciousness of the people of Europe and the declining prestige of the popes. Because of his leaving the silence of his cell to take up a hand-to-hand fight with the vices of his time, posterity is deprived of the philosophical books of his more ma-

ture years. Sharing the sorrow with all who regret the
loss which the "calm and obscure regions of Philosophy" suffered by Ockham's entering the political
arena, we may discover in his active adventures a new
light which puts his impressive personality in even
more favorable relief.

A man with such empirical bent as Ockham possessed
was predisposed to take an active part in life in some
form or other. It was unavoidable for one of his temperament to go out into the dusty welter of life to experience the rhythm of that reality whose bases he had
discovered in his own indomitable will. In the thick
of conflicting interests he identified himself with what
he thought to be highest. In his fights for the dream
of the Spirituals or for a more ideal church life he
tried to raise the torch of light. His tireless labors give
an eloquent proof of the fact that philosophy for him
was not merely a theory but a matter of life and death.
Although a lone fighter, throughout his wanderings he
had found strength and a promise of triumph in the
conviction expressed in the following words:

> In matters of faith and of science I am more im-
> pressed by one evident reason or by one authori-
> tative passage of the Holy Writ correctly under-
> stood than by the common chorus of mankind. I
> am not ashamed to be convinced by truth. In fact,
> to have truth victorious over me I estimate the
> most useful thing for me. But I never want to be
> defeated by the multitude. For I consider an open
> heresy the allegation of many that I should not
> oppose the multitude. It may, indeed, be read in
> the sacred utterances that the multitude, as a rule,
> errs, and that very often one solitary man may put
> all the rest to flight.[15]

[15] Brampton, op. cit.; Proem. 6.

PART TWO

SELECTIONS

LOGIC

Ockham devoted the major part of his interest to problems of logic. The following translations are representative chapters taken from his voluminous *Summa totius logicae*. The significance of this outstanding logical work of the Middle Ages consists in a critical transformation of the *logica antiqua*, that is, of the Aristotelian logic in its *Porphyrian-Boethian* rendition, in terms of the *logica nova*, that is, in terms of the significatory and suppositional logic of Petrus Hispanus. Ockham's analysis of the forms of discourse in this new light yielded a nominalistic logic. Logical predication is significa-tion. The categories of Aristotle are not ontological realities but entities of reason predicable of external things. Logic is essentially formal, a *scientia sermocinalis*. How far Ockham was successful in reinterpreting Aristotle as a nominalist and supplanting the view which held and holds the Stagirite as a moderate realist, only renewed critical efforts undertaken by experts can decide.

PART I. CHAPTER 1.

A LL WHO treat of Logic intend to establish by arguments that syllogisms are composed of propositions, and propositions of terms.[0] A term, therefore, is nothing else than the extreme part[1] of a proposition. For Aristotle, defining the term, says in the First Part of the *Prior Analytics*: I call a term that into which a proposition is resolved, such as the predicate or that of which the predicate is stated by adding or removing the "is" or the "is not." But, although every term is called the extreme part of a proposition, or may become such, not all terms are of the same nature. For that reason, to obtain a perfect knowledge of terms we have first to get acquainted with certain distinctions of terms.

It is to be known, then, that to follow Boethius in

[0] I. e., terminus (boundary, end) because propositions are resolved ultimately into words which in this terminating rôle are called terms.

[1] I. e., the subject or predicate, the "extrema propositionis."

the first part of his *On Interpretation,* just as there are
three kinds of discourse: written, spoken, and conceived, this latter being in the mind only; in the same
manner, the term, too, is threefold: written, spoken,
and conceived. The written term is a part of a written
proposition, which is seen, or may be seen, with the
physical eye. The spoken term is a part of the proposition pronounced by the mouth and meant to be heard
by physical hearing. The conceived term is an intention, or passion of the soul, which by its nature signifies or co-signifies something, and is meant to be a part
of a mental proposition. Now these conceived terms
and the propositions composed of them are those mental words which Saint Augustine says in the fifth book
On the Trinity to be of no language. These words remain in the mind only and cannot be brought to light
externally, although words, as signs subordinated to
them, are pronounced externally. For we call words
signs subordinated to concepts or intentions of the
soul. The word "sign" is not used here in the proper
sense, as if words signify concepts originally and properly speaking. Rather we mean to imply that words
are used to signify those same things that are signified
by the concepts of the mind, in such manner that first
the concept signifies something naturally, and secondly
the word signifies that same thing. And the depen-
dence goes so far that the word, after it was instituted
to signify something which is signified by the concept
of the mind, should that concept change its signified
object, at the same time the word, too, without a new
institution would also change its signified object. And
to this fact can be referred Aristotle's statement that
words are marks of such passions which are in the
soul. This is also the meaning of Boethius' statement

that words signify concepts; and, generally, the same is meant by all authors who say that words signify the passions of the soul, or are marks of them. Their intention is nothing else than to say that words are signs which signify secondarily those things that are primarily presented by the passions. To be sure, some words present primarily certain passions of the soul or concepts, which words, however, secondarily, present other intentions of the soul, as we shall show later. And what was said of words with regard to passions, intentions, or concepts, can be said similarly about written signs with reference to words.

Now these terms present certain differences. One is that the concept or the passion of the soul naturally signifies whatever it signifies. The pronounced or written term, on the other hand, does not signify anything save by voluntary institution. From this fact another difference follows, namely, that the spoken or written term can change its signified object at discretion, whereas the concept-term never changes its signification at anyone's pleasure. For the sake of those who are not initiated, it is to be known that "sign" is taken in a twofold manner, in one way for anything that, as apprehended, conveys something else to cognition.[2] To be sure, the sign does not lead to the first cognition of the object, as it is shown elsewhere. It leads to the actual knowledge of what has been previously known. And in this way it signifies something naturally, as every effect signifies at least its own cause. Thus, the disk signifies wine in the taven. However, I am not speaking of the sign as generally used. To

---

[2] Sometimes called "signum manifestativum," because it manifests the existence of something, e. g., fossils in geological strata, a past life; clouds, a coming storm.

use that word in another way, the sign is taken for
that which conveys something to cognition and is
meant to stand for that thing[3] or which is to be
added in a proposition, such as syncategorematic
words,[4] verbs, and other parts of speech which do not
have a definite signification. "Sign" is also everything
which is meant to be compounded out of these parts,
such as discourse or the proposition. Taking the word
"sign" in this sense, the word is not a natural sign for
anything.

CHAPTER 2.

It is to be known that this word "term" is used in a
threefold manner. In one way, "term" is taken for
everything which can be the copula or the extreme of
a categorical proposition, that is, subject or predicate
or the determination of the extreme or of the verb. In
this way even a proposition can be a term, as it can
be part of a proposition. This is one example: " 'man
is an animal' is a proposition." Here this proposition,
"man is an animal," is subject and "a proposition" is
predicate. The word "term" is used in a second way
when it is distinguished from discourse (*oratio*). And
in this way all incomplexa[1] are called terms. This was
my way of using the word term in the previous chapter. In a third way it is used precisely and more strictly
for that which, taken in a significatory manner, can
be the subject or the predicate of some proposition. In

[3] Sometimes called "signum suppositivum" because it is substituted for a signified thing and plays its part.

[4] I. e., words which must be added to another word in the
nominative case if we want to use them in a proposition, e. g.,
every, all, each.

[1] I. e., irreducible elements of speech as "man": "homo,"
which cannot be further reduced to ho and mo so as to give a
meaning.

this usage no verb, no conjunction, no adverb, no interjection is a term. There are many words also, such as the syncategorematic words, which cannot be terms, because such words, although they could be the extremes of a proposition if they are taken materially or simply,[2] yet when they are taken in a significatory manner cannot be the extremes of propositions. Therefore this discourse: "reads (*legit*) is a verb," is congruous and right, if this verb "reads" is taken materially. If, however, this verb is taken in a significatory manner the discourse is not intelligible. The case is the same in such examples as "all (*omnis*) is a word"; "once (*olim*) is an adverb"; "if (*si*) is a conjunction"; "from (*ab*) is a preposition." Now the Philosopher does not use the word "term" in this manner in the first book of the *Prior Analytics*.

In this sense of the word, not only one incomplex (expression) can be a term, taking term in this fashion, but also a compound of two incomplex (expressions) as (the expression) compounded of an adjective and a substantive and (the expression) compounded of an adverb and a participle, or of a proposition with a part of speech in its proper case, can be a term just as the subject or a predicate of a proposition can likewise be a term. For in this proposition: "white man is a man," neither "man" nor "white" is the subject, but this whole, "white man." In the same manner, in the proposition "this fast running (person) is a man" (*hic currens velociter est homo*), neither "running (person) nor "fast" is the subject but the whole "fast running (person)."

It is to be known, further, that not only a noun em-

[2] These technical terms are later explained, in the sixty-fourth chapter of the Logic.

ployed in the nominative case can be a term, but one
employed in the oblique cases[3] also, because such nouns,
too, can be subject or predicate of a proposition. However, an oblique case cannot be the subject with regard to any verb. It is not properly said, "of the man
sees the donkey" (*hominis videt asinum*), although it
would be proper to say, "the donkey is a property of
the man" (*hominis esse asinus*). But how, and with
reference to which verbs, an oblique case can be a subject and with reference to which verbs it cannot, is the
task of the grammarian to consider, for it is his business to consider the constructions of words.

Chapter 11.*

Since we have discussed the divisions which may belong both to (mental) terms which signify naturally
and to those terms which are arbitrarily instituted, we
have to say something about some of the divisions
which belong to terms instituted at pleasure. The first
division is this. Some of the voluntarily instituted
terms are words of first imposition, some are words of
second imposition. Words of second imposition are
words which are employed to signify such signs as are
instituted at pleasure and those things which go with
such signs, but only as long as they are signs. But
this general term of second imposition may be taken in
a twofold manner. First, in a broad sense; in which
case everything is a word of second imposition which
signifies words instituted voluntarily; instituted voluntarily they need to be[1] whether or not the word of second imposition be related to the intentions of the soul

---

[3] I. e., all cases but the nominative and the vocative.

* Cf. Appendix, pp. 202-203.

[1] In the original: "sed non nisi quando sunt ad placitum in-
stituta."

which are natural signs. Words of this kind are such
words as "noun," "pronoun," "conjunction," "verb,"
"case," "number," "mode," "tense," and the like employed as the grammarian uses them. And these are
called 'names of names' because they are employed to
signify parts of discourse, but only as long as such parts
are significatory. Words, however, which may be employed for terms both when they are not significatory
and when they are significatory are not called words of
second imposition. And, therefore, such terms (*nomina*) as "quality," "pronounced word," and the like,
although they signify words (*voces*) instituted at
pleasure and are verified with reference to them, yet,
because they would signify words instituted at pleasure even if these were not significatory as they now
are, such terms are not words of second imposition. On the other hand, "noun" is a word of second
imposition, because the word "man" of itself, before it
was employed for signification, was not a noun; in the
same manner, "of man" (*hominis*), before it was employed for signification, was of no case, the same being true of other words of this kind.

Strictly speaking, however, we call a word one of
second imposition when it signifies only arbitrarily instituted signs. Such a word has nothing to do with the
intentions of the soul, which are natural signs. To
words of this class belong such examples as "declen-
sion," "conjugation," and the like. Any other word,
that is, words not of second imposition either in one
or in the other way, are called words of first imposition. To be sure, the name of first imposition may be
taken in a twofold manner. First, widely, and in this
way all words not of second imposition are words of
first imposition. In that sense, such syncategorematic

signs as "all," "nobody," "somebody," "anybody," and
the like, are words of first imposition. Second, it may
be taken strictly, and then only the categorematic words
which are not words of second imposition are called
words of first imposition. Now the words of first imposition, in the strict sense, are divided into two groups,
called terms of first intention, and terms of second intention. Terms of second intention are called those
which are employed precisely for the signification of
the intentions of the soul, which are natural signs, and
of other signs which are arbitrarily instituted or go
with such signs. And such terms are "genus," "species," "universal," "particular," and the like. Terms
of this class are nothing else but intentions of the soul,
which are natural signs, or their arbitrarily instituted
signs. Therefore, it may be said that this common
term of second intention may be taken strictly and
largely. In a wide sense we call something a term of
second intention when it signifies the intentions of the
soul which are natural signs, whether it also signifies
arbitrarily instituted signs, while they are signs, or it
does not thus signify them. In this manner some terms
of second intention are also words of second imposition. In a strict sense, however, only that is called a
term of second intention which precisely signifies the
intentions of the soul, which are natural signs. Taking the term of second intention in this sense, no such
term is a word of second imposition. Terms of first
intention, on the other hand, are all terms that differ
from the afore-mentioned class in that they signify
some things that are neither signs nor go with such
signs. To this class belong such names as "man,"
"animal," "Socrates," "Plato," "whiteness," "white,"
"good," "true," and the like. Some of these terms

signify precisely things that are not signs meant to
stand for things; others again signify signs and at the
same time signify other things also.[2]

From all this it can be inferred that certain terms
signify precisely signs which are instituted at pleasure,
but only as long as they are signs;[3] certain other terms
again, signify both arbitrarily instituted signs and natural ones;[4] finally, certain terms signify precisely things
which are not such signs as are parts of a proposition,[5]
while certain others, again, signify such things which
are not parts of a proposition or discourse and their
respective signs also.[6] Terms of this kind are "thing,"
"being," "something," and similar others.

Chapter 12.

Because it was said in the preceding chapter that
some names are those of first intention and some of
second intention, and because the ignorance of words
is for many people an occasion to err, for that reason,
it is to be incidentally noted, what is intention, what is
first and second intention, and how they are distinguished. First, then, we have to know that "intention
of the soul" is the name given to an entity in the soul
which is meant to signify something. And as was said
before in connection with writing, which was found
to be a secondary sign of the word, in the same manner, words, which are the foremost of all arbitrarily

[2] In the original: "quorum aliqua significant precise res quae
non sunt signa, nata supponere pro illis: aliqua vero significant
talia signa et simul cum hoc alias res."

[3] Words of second imposition in the strict sense.

[4] Second intentions in the wide sense.

[5] First intentions in the strict sense.

[6] The "transcendentals," that is, the six all-pervasive attributes of being characteristic of any datum of experience: "being," "thing," "something," "unity," "truth," "goodness."

instituted signs, are secondary signs, of those things
of which the intentions of the soul are primary signs.
It is with reference to this that Aristotle says that
words are marks of those passions which are in the
soul. Now this something subsisting in the soul, which
is a sign of the thing, and out of which the mental
proposition is composed as the vocal proposition is composed out of the words, is called sometimes the intention of the soul, sometimes the concept of the soul,
sometimes the passion of the soul, and sometimes a
likeness of the thing. Boethius in his Commentary on
the book *On Interpretation* calls it the meaning (*intellectus*). And he adds that the mental proposition is
composed of "meanings," not of such meanings as are
actually identical with the intellectual soul, but of intentions, which are certain signs in the soul signifying
some things, I mean intentions, out of which mental
propositions are composed. Therefore, when somebody pronounces a vocal proposition, he first formu-
lates internally a mental proposition which is of no
language, as is evidenced by the fact that many people
frequently form inner propositions which, however,
they cannot express because of linguistic shortcomings.
The parts of such mental propositions are called concepts, intentions, similitudes, and meanings. But what
is that in the soul which is such a sign? It must be said
that there are various opinions about this question.
Some say that it is nothing else than some fictitious
entity produced by the soul; some say that it is a certain quality subsisting psychologically in the soul, distinct from the act of understanding; again some say
that it is the act of understanding itself. And for this
latter view the following reason may be shown: it is
needless to have recourse to many entities when we can

get along with fewer ones. Everything, however, that can be saved by admitting something distinct from the act of understanding, could be saved without such a distinct thing. For to stand for something and to signify something can be attributed just as well to the act of understanding as to that fictitious entity; therefore, there is no need to posit anything else beyond the act of understanding.

These opinions will be examined below. For the time being it should be sufficient to say that the intention is something in the soul, a sign naturally signifying an object for which it can stand, something which may be part of a mental proposition. Such intention is twofold: the first is the sign of something not itself a sign, whether that sign signifies the object generally or not. This is called the first intention, such as the intention of the soul which can be predicated of all white things, and so on. However, it is to be known that the first intention is taken in a twofold manner, strictly and widely. Widely, we call first intention any intentional sign subsisting in the soul which does not precisely signify intentions or signs. And it does not make any difference whether we take "sign" in a strict sense of the word, that is, for everything that signifies so as to stand for its signified object in a proposition; or whether we take sign in a wide sense, that is, in the way in which we stated that the syncategorematic words signify. In this latter sense mental verbs and mental syncategorematic words, adverbs, conjunctions, and the like, may be called first intentions. Strictly speaking, however, we call first intention a mental term meant to stand for its signified object. The second intention, on the other hand, is that which is the sign of such first intentions. And to this class belong such intentions as genus, species, and others of this kind. For just as we predicate an intention with reference to all men, because it is common to all men, by saying "this man is a man," "that man is a man," and "that other man is a man," and so on regarding every single man; in the same manner, we predicate with reference to all intentions which signify and stand for things that are not signs, an intention which is common to them by saying: "this species is a species," and "that species is a species," and so on. Similarly when we say: "animal is a genus," "stone is a genus," "color is a genus," and so on, we predicate an intention about intentions. By saying, then: "man is a name," "whiteness is a name," we predicate a name about different names, and therefore, as the words of second impositions signify at pleasure the words of first imposition, in the same manner, the second intention naturally signifies the first. And as the word of first imposition signifies other things than words, in the same manner the first intention signifies other things than intentions. It can also be said that the second intention may be taken strictly for the intention which precisely signifies first intentions, or widely, for the intention which signifies intentions and arbitrarily instituted signs, if there are such second intentions.

CHAPTER 41.

After the preceding it remains to discuss the terms inferior to (the term) "being," which constitute the ten categories. It is to be known that the name "category" is one of second imposition or intention, such as the name "genus," although the entities of which it is predicated are incomplex terms of first intention. Category, however, is taken in a twofold manner. In one way it is taken for the total order of certain things arranged according to higher and lower. In another way it is taken for the primary and most general element in such order. And taken in this manner, every category is an incomplex term of first intention signifying things which are not signs. When, however, category is taken in the first manner, it may be said that in an order so arranged there are incomplex terms of first intention and some incomplex terms of second intention. Or it may be said that some of these incomplex terms are of first, some of second intention. For according to the opinion which states that the intention or concept is a quality, psychologically[1] existing in the mind, this general term "genus" belongs under the category of quality or relation. That is, according to this view, every "genus" is a quality, and this general term "genus" is a second intention or the name of a second intention, while the general term "color" is a first intention. Many similar cases might be cited.

It may be objected, however, that a first intention is not superior to a second intention; or that a first intention is not predicated of a second intention nor conversely; or that an entity of reason cannot belong to a category of real existents, but that a second intention is an entity of reason, and, consequently, does not belong under a category of real existents.

To the first of these objections it is to be answered that a first intention *is*[2] superior to a second intention; as, for instance, "being" is a first intention, and yet it is superior to a second intention, for every second intention is an entity, but not conversely.

---

[1] "subjective" in the original; i. e., existing in the mind as in a subject.

[2] Italics mine.

To the second objection this is the answer. It is true that a first intention is not predicated of a second intention when both of these intentions stand for themselves, for, in that case, it would have to be granted that a second intention is a first intention, a proposition which is false. However, a first intention can be predicated of a second intention, that is, not standing for itself. For that reason this proposition "genus is a quality" is a true one, and yet this category, "quality," is not predicated as standing for itself, but for the second intention which is the term "genus." Similarly in this spoken proposition "noun is a quality," a word of first imposition is being predicated of a word of second imposition, that is, not as standing for itself but as standing for a word of second imposition; and yet no word of second imposition is a word of first imposition.

To the third objection we may answer that belonging under a category is taken in a twofold manner. In one way something may belong under a category in such a manner that the first[3] of that category taken in a significatory manner is predicated of the demonstrative pronoun pointing out this thing. Taking the notion of belonging under a category in this sense, there is nothing under the genus of substance but the particular substance, because every substance is a particular substance. Again, in this sense of belonging under a category, all universals which precisely indicate substances belong under the category of quality, because every universal is a quality. In another way something may belong under a category in such a manner that the first (the most general term) of that category taken in a

[3] I. e., the most general term; e. g., "substance" is the first term of the category of substance, in which "animal," "man," and other less general terms are also included.

significatory manner is predicated of it taken in a significatory manner. Thus, some universals belong under the genus of substance because substance is predicated of certain universals taken in a significatory manner, for instance, by saying "every stone is a substance"; "every man is a substance"; "every animal is a substance"; and so on. Therefore, the assumption that "an entity of reason cannot be in a category of real things" is false, whether we accept the notion of belonging under a category in one way or the other.

To be sure, it is to be known that according to the above mentioned view which states that an intention, concept, or passion of the soul is a quality of the mind, a thing is regarded as an entity of the reason not because this entity is not a real thing existing in the natural world; but it is regarded as an entity of reason because it is nowhere else but in the reason, being used by the mind for something else or being a thing whereby the mind understands something else. Thus, all propositions and conclusions and mental terms are entities of reason, and yet they do exist truly and really in the natural world; in fact, they are more perfect and more real entities than any corporeal qualities. And, therefore, when the Commentator and the Philosopher divide "being" into "real being" and "rational being," or into "entity in the soul" and "entity outside of the soul," and, then, afterwards, divide "real being" into the ten categories, this division is made not by simple opposition as when "animal" is divided into "rational animal" and "irrational animal," but rather by a division of the signification of the word; as when the Philosopher in the First Part of the *Prior Analytics* divides the contingent into "necessary contingent" and into "indefinite contingent" and "the possible" in general. And, therefore, as one of those three members of the division is predicated of the rest—the following sentences being true: "The necessary contingent is possible." "The indefinite contingent is possible."—in the same manner, regardless of the above division of being, this is true: "An entity of reason is a real entity," taking the term "real" for something which is a veritable quality existing in the natural world.

And if, by real entity or by an entity outside of the soul, we understand an entity which is not in the soul, then, the division of real being into ten categories is not a division of being in its "inferiora" but is similar and equivalent to a division according to which some real entity outside of the soul is indicated by *this*[4] category, some by *another,*[4] and so on. Or the above division is similar to saying that the real entity outside of the soul is either in *such*[4] or in *such*[4] a category; and so with the rest. But having said all this we do not deny that these categories include many entities which are not entities outside of the soul.

CHAPTER 43.

Having treated certain general aspects with reference to the categories, although many other things can be said, it remains to speak specifically of each, and, in the first place, of substance. Concerning this, it is to be known, first, that "substance" is understood in a great many ways. In one way, any thing is called a substance which is distinguished from all other things. In that sense, we find the term used often by authors talking about the substance of whiteness, the substance of color, and so with the rest. In another way, substance is taken more strictly as every thing which is

[4] Italics mine.

not an accident. Thus, we apply the term substance both to matter and form and to the composite resulting from the two. Again, in another way, and this is the strictest sense of the word, substance is called every thing that is not accident, that does not inhere in something else, and that is not an essential part of something. In this sense substance is understood as a most general genus, divided by Aristotle into primary and secondary substances. However, this is not to be understood as if this division were of some general term predicable *per se* of these divisions, or of demonstrative pronouns indicating these dividing parts. For by pointing to any secondary substance this proposition is false: "man is a substance"; contrarily this proposition is true: "no substance is secondary substance." This is evident from the preceding. For it was said before that no universal is a substance, but every secondary substance is a universal because it is a genus, or species. According to Aristotle, therefore, no secondary substance is substance. Again according to the doctrine of Aristotle, whatever is negated of all parts, subsumed under something general, is negated universally of that general something also. But secondary substance is negated universally regarding all parts subsumed under substance; consequently it is negated universally of substance. This proposition, then, is true: "no substance is secondary substance"; consequently this proposition also: "no secondary substance is substance." The assumption[1] is evident. For this proposition: "no corporeal substance is secondary substance" is true, and similarly this one also: "no incorporeal substance is secondary substance." That the first proposition and also the second is true is evident by virtue of the same

[1] I. e., the major premise.

rule. For this proposition: "No animate body is secondary substance" is true; in the same manner the following also: "no inanimate body is secondary substance." That the first proposition is true is evident because no inanimate, insensitive body is secondary substance; and in the same manner, no animate, sensitive body is secondary substance. The truth of the first of these propositions can be proved by the same rule. For this proposition: "no animate, sensitive, rational body is secondary substance" is true, and on the same ground this proposition also: "no animate, sensitive, irrational body is secondary substance." The truth of the first of these propositions is evident, because its converse: "no man is a secondary substance" is true, which is, of course, evident because any singular proposition (contained under it) is true. It remains, therefore, that according to the doctrine of Aristotle the proposition: "no substance is a secondary substance" is without qualification true. Pointing out, therefore, any (secondary) substance, the statement, "this is a substance," is without qualification false. We have to state, then, that the aforementioned division is only the division of a general term into less general, and is equivalent to the following division: Of terms which introduce or signify substances outside of the soul, some are names proper to one substance and those names are called primary substances; some, however, are names common to many substances and they are called secondary substances, these names being in turn divided because some are genera, some are species. All of them, to be sure, are in truth qualities and, therefore, all secondary substances belong under the category of quality—meaning thereby that quality is predicated of the demonstrative pronoun indicating that thing. However, these secondary substances belong under the category of substance, meaning by this the thing of which, taking it in a significatory manner, the term substance is predicated. For that reason, in this proposition: "man is an animal" or "man is a substance," the term "man" does not stand for itself but for its signified object. If it stood for itself, this proposition: "man is a substance" would be false and this proposition: "man is a quality" would be true. In the same manner, if the spoken word "man" stood for itself, this proposition: "man is a substance" would be false and the proposition "man is a word" would be true. From all this it is evident that secondary substances are nothing but certain names and qualities signifying precisely substances; and for that and for no other reason, they are said to be in the category of substance.

This view is in accordance with the statements of authorities. The Philosopher in his *On the Categories* says that every substance seems to signify a "this something," and as to the primary substances it is undoubtedly true that it signifies a "this something." From this it is manifest that in the conception of Aristotle "primary substance" signifies a "this something," but the particular substance which exists outside of the soul does not signify a "this something" but it is the thing which is signified. Aristotle, then, at this point calls substance the name of a particular substance which is outside of the soul, and on the same ground and *a fortiori,* he has to call those names secondary substances.

In the same way Boethius in different places in his commentary to *On the Categories* says that the Philosopher in the first book treats of words and consequently, calls those words primary and secondary substances. Similarly, Aristotle says that the primary and secondary substances are in the category of substance, and he there states that the things which are in a category are incomplex terms out of which propositions are formed. But propositions are not formed out of substances which exist outside of the soul; therefore, etc.* Damascenus, too, states that words are grouped within the category of substance. There is, then, a uniformity in the statements of the ancients who say that Aristotle calls the common names of substances secondary substances.

The view of Aristotle, that species are substances in a more eminent sense than genera are, does not create any difficulty. By such propositions he does not mean anything except that, to the question "What is it?" asked of a substance which is pointed to, a more appropriate answer can be given by the species than by the genus. And, therefore, such a proposition: "the species rather than the genus is substance" is false in a literal sense, but is true according as the Philosopher understood it. It is, then, to be said without qualification that the division discussed is a division into names —some of which are proper, some common. Proper names are called primary substances; common names are called secondary substances.

Nevertheless, it should be known that the Philosopher uses the name "primary substance" equivocally. For he sometimes uses the term for the names of substances which exist outside of the soul, as when he says: "all substance appears to signify a 'this something.'" In another way does he use the terms for the

* "Etc." in this connection stands for an abbreviated form of the conclusion.

substances themselves which exist outside of the soul, as when he says: "substance is that which is said properly, principally and chiefly to underlie." Therefore, when the Philosopher says that all other things are either enunciated of the primary substances or are inherent in the substances, he is not talking about substances which actually underlie but about the subjects of propositions. This is why Damascenus says in his *Logic,* chapter IX, that "subject" is taken in a twofold manner, viz., according to existence, and in this sense the substance which exists outside of the soul as singular, is subject to the accidents; or it is taken according to a proposition, and in this sense the particular is subject to the universal. And the Philosopher uses in this latter way the term "subject" when he says that secondary substance is that which is predicated of a subject and, thus, primary substances are not really subsisting things subject to secondary substances, but are subjects by way of propositions.

From this it is apparent that when the Philosopher says that the secondary substances are enunciated of the primary substances as of subjects, this cannot be except by way of a proposition. The primary substance, then, is the subject in predication and the secondary subject is the predicate. But no proposition is formed from substances which are outside of the soul; therefore, the primary substance, that is, the subject of a proposition with respect to the secondary substance, is not a substance which exists outside of the soul.

Accordingly, when Aristotle says that if the primary substances were destroyed all else would be destroyed also, he does not mean a real destruction or real construction but he thinks of destruction by means of a proposition, i. e., by a negative proposition. In this sense, when actual existence is not predicated of some member which belongs under the common term "substance," then, actual existence is truly denied of that common term, of its proper accidents and of the properties of that common term. However, in that, he simply means that such inferences as the following are valid: "this man does not exist," "this man does not exist," and "this man does not exist," and so on with the rest; therefore, "no man exists"; therefore, nothing can be seen and so with others (examples).[2] Now if he meant a real destruction he would commit a fallacy. For even if no stone existed, for all that this genus "stone" could remain and somebody could form this proposition: "no man is a stone," which would be impossible unless the parts of the proposition existed. Consequently, that certain genus "stone" would at that time exist even though it would not be predicated affirmatively of anything in an assertoric[3] proposition of present time.[4]

[2] I owe thanks to Dr. Ernest A. Moody for the solution of this difficult passage. As he states this sentence is the tail end of another example of such a *consequentia*, the first part of which had been omitted accidentally from the text. The full text would be: "this visible thing does not exist" and "this visible thing does not exist," and so on with the rest; therefore . . .

[3] assertoric, i. e., asserting existence.

[4] In the original: "et per consequens hoc genus lapis esset tunc et tamen de nullo affirmative predicaretur in propositione mere deinesse et mere de praesenti."

The following two chapters constitute Ockham's doctrine of supposition, an intimate understanding of which will throw a great light on problems related to the philosophy of language, the symbolism of the mind, logical positivism, and to the unification of the sciences. By supposition Ockham means the usage of a term according to a certain signification as determined by the context of speech. The signification of terms as long as they are out of context is more or less undetermined and admits of a great variety of use. One and the same term may signify in a multifarious manner changing its mode of signification as a diamond changes colors (supposition) according to the diamond's various positions (proposition). The univocal, equivocal, and analogous usage of one and the same term may bring this quality of terms clearly to mind. The peculiar modality of signification which a term acquires when it stands in the context of a certain proposition is called by Ockham supposition. For instance when we say "men are mortal" and, then, "men constitute the human race," the mode of signification in the first sentence where the term "men" signifies distributively differs from that in the second sentence where the same term signifies collectively. This particular determinateness of signification is what we mean by supposition. It can be noted in the following two chapters that the most typical supposition is that of personal supposition in which a term strictly signifies a signified object (*significatum*) and thus supposits for it. In the simple and material supposition the term represents either its own underlying meaning as when we say "man is a species" ("man" the term symbolizes the meaning of man) or it represents itself as when we say " 'man' is a noun" ("man" the term introduces itself as a term). Although simple and material suppositions do not involve cases of strict signification because the word "signification" is restricted to the symbolization of some object, in a subordinate sense, these two types also may be considered as particular modes of signification and, thus, may be included as genuine suppositions.

CHAPTER 63.

After the signification of terms it remains to treat of the supposition, which is a property of the term but only in a proposition. First, it is to be known that we take supposition in a twofold manner, that is, widely and strictly. Taken widely, it is not distinguished from appellation,[1] because appellation belongs under supposi-

---

[1] I. e., from the predication of an attribute with reference to a term. For instance, in the sentence "Alexander was great," "greatness" is attributed to the term "Alexander."

tion. Taken strictly, it is distinguished from appellation. My intention is not to treat of supposition in this
second but in the first sense; and in this (wider) sense
both the subject and the predicate equally supposit, and
generally anything supposits which may be the subject
or predicate of a proposition.

By supposition we mean the position (or substitution) for other things so that when a term in a proposition stands for something we employ that term for
that something. That term or the nominative case of
the term if it is in an oblique[2] case, is, then, verified by
that something[3] without the help of a demonstrative
pronoun and, thus, the term supposits for that thing.
If the term is a subject it is denoted by way of a proposition that that something[4] or a pronoun pointing it out
is predicated of the term. If, on the other hand, the
term which supposits is a predicate, it will be denoted
that the subject about which the proposition is being
formed, or the pronoun pointing out the subject, is to
be subsumed with regard to that predicate. Thus, when
we say, "man is an animal," we denote that Socrates is
an animal, so that this proposition would be true if it is
formed by pointing out Socrates. By the following
proposition, however, "man is a noun," it is denoted
that the word "man" stands for that word (i. e., noun).
In the same manner, in this proposition "the white
thing (*album*) is an animal," it is denoted that the thing
which is white is an animal so that this proposition is

[2] I. e., any of the cases except the nominative or vocative case.

[3] Verification here means the establishing of the truly significatory character of the term.

[4] I. e., the "significatum," the signified content of the term
which may be either something general or something concrete
and particular.

true "this is an animal," pointing out that thing which is white, and for that reason the subject supposits for that thing (animal).[5] And the same thing is to be said with reference to a predicate. For by the proposition "Socrates is white," it is denoted that Socrates is that thing to which whiteness belongs. And if no other thing possessed whiteness save Socrates then the predicate would precisely supposit for Socrates.

Now there is a general rule according to which the term in a proposition, at least when it is taken in a significatory manner, never supposits for anything unless it is truly predicated of it. From this it follows that it is falsely stated by some who are ignorant that the concrete term representing the predicate stands for the (universal) form. That is, that in the following proposition: "Socrates is white," white stands for whiteness. This is simply false. Whiteness is white, no matter how the terms supposit, and therefore, according to the teaching of Aristotle such a concrete term can never stand for such form signified through its abstract term. In case of other concrete terms, however, about which we have been discoursing, this is quite possible. In the same manner, in this proposition: "Man is god," "man" stands legitimately for the son of God, because he is really a man.

CHAPTER 64.

At the outset we have to know that supposition is divided into simple, personal, and material supposition. The personal supposition generally means that a term stands for its signified object, whether that signified object be a thing outside of the soul, or a word,

[5] That is, the term "white thing" (*album*), signifies in the particular mode of suppositing or standing for an animal.

or an intention of the soul, or something written, or any
other imaginable thing. Whenever such a term is subject or predicate in a proposition it always stands for
its signified object and is used in a significatory manner. Examples for personal supposition are the following: (for the first instance) "man is an animal";
here "man" stands for its signified objects, because it
is employed only to signify men in particular and it
does not signify something common to them but the
single individuals themselves as Damascenus[1] teaches.
An example for the second instance is this: "every
noun is a part of discourse." Here "noun" stands for
words exclusively, for when we employ it to signify, it
is employed for the signification of those words. To
give an example for the third instance: "every species
is a universal," or "every intention of the soul is in
the soul." Here both subjects supposit personally because they stand for those things for which they are
employed to signify. An example of the the fourth
instance would be: "every written discourse (*dictio*)
is a discourse"; here the subject supposits for nothing
else but for its signified objects, that is, for written
things, and, therefore, it supposits personally. From
this it can be seen that the personal supposition is adequately described by those who say that in personal
supposition the term stands for its signified object and
is used in a significatory manner.

The simple supposition is that in which the term
stands for the intention of the soul but not in a significative way, e. g., "man is a species." This term
"man" stands for the intention of the soul, because that

---

[1] St. John Damascene (died around 749 A. D.) Greek monk
and church father whose *Fountain of Knowledge* was one of the
earliest sources of Aristotelian logic and ontology.

intention is the "species." Properly speaking, however, the term "man" does not signify that intention, since the word and the intention of the soul are only subordinately significative in the process of signification, according to the manner which was expounded at another place.[2] From this it can be seen how false is the general opinion which states that the term in a simple supposition stands for its signified object, because in simple supposition the term stands for the intention of the soul which, properly speaking, is not the signified object (*significatum*) of the term. The kind of term they are talking about signifies real things and not intentions of the soul.

The material supposition is that in which the term does not function in a significative way, but stands either for the word or for the writing as can be seen in this example: "man is a noun"; here "man" stands for itself and yet it does not signify itself. In the same manner when we say "man is being written," here is a case of material supposition, because the term stands for that which is being written.

It is to be known that as this threefold supposition belongs to the spoken word, in the same manner, it may belong to the written word (*dictio*) also. Therefore, if the above-mentioned four propositions: "man is an animal"; "man is a species"; "man is a monosyllabic word"; "man is a written sign" (*dictio*); will be put down in writing, every one of them may be verified, taken, of course, every one for itself, for "animal" in

---

[2] Allusion to the following passage in Chapter I: "The word 'sign' is not used here in the proper sense, as if words signify concepts originally and properly speaking. Rather we mean to imply that words are used to signify those same things that are signified by the concepts of the mind, in such manner that first the concept signifies something naturally, and secondly the word signifies that same thing."

no way could be "species," nor "monosyllabic word," nor "written sign" (*dictio*). In the same manner that which is "species" is not "animal," nor "monosyllabic word," etc. To be sure in the last two propositions the term has a material supposition, although the supposition could be distinguished according as the term stands for the word or the written sign. Thus, if they were functioning in employment, we would have two diverse species of supposition, comparable to the case when we distinguish between suppositions standing for a word and standing for a signified object (*significatum*); or when we distinguish a supposition standing for a signified object from that standing for an intention. And the same diversity of supposition which may belong to the spoken and written term could also belong to the concept-term if the intention is taken as standing for that which signifies for its own behalf, and for the word, and for the written sign. One of these suppositions I would call personal, an other one simple, and an other material. It is also to be known that we do not call the personal supposition personal because it stands for a person; neither do we call the simple supposition simple because it stands for something simple; nor the material one material as if it would stand for matter. This denomination is employed because of the reasons mentioned before. The terms material, simple, personal are used in logic and in the other sciences by equivocation. However, we do not use them in logic frequently except when we add the word "supposition."

THEORY OF KNOWLEDGE
AND
METAPHYSICS

Ockham's nominalistic epistemology, by banishing the universal from ontology into the domain of logic and insisting on the individual character of all reality, fatally undermined the scholastic structure and initiated the line of thought which paved the road toward modern empiricism and ultimately to modern idealism. As a result the possibility of metaphysics, that is, the possibility of the knowledge of reality as such, became the crucial point of philosophy.

A NY IMAGINABLE thing which exists by itself without any addition, is singular and numerically one.[1] Every science begins with individuals. From sensation, which gives only singular things, arises memory, from memory experience, and through experience, we obtain the universal which is the basis of art and science. As all our knowledge derives from the senses, every science, too, originates from individual objects, although no doctrine should treat of singular things. Properly speaking, that is, there is no science of individuals but of universals standing for individuals.[2]

I say that no intellectual act is without a phantasm, for the reason that all intellectual cognition necessarily presupposes in our present status sensitive imagination both of the exterior and interior senses.[3] Nothing can be an object of the interior sense without having been an object of the exterior sense.[4] Intuitive cognition is cognition by virtue of which it can be known that a thing is when it is, and that a thing is not when it is

[1] *Expos. aur.*, Praedicab., Proem.
[2] *Expos. aurea*, Praedicab., De specie.
[3] *Sent.*, Prol., qu. 1, V. V.
[4] *Sent.* IV, qu. 12, K.

not.[5] When someone sees Socrates intuitively and
whiteness as inherent in Socrates, he can know plainly
that Socrates is white.[6]

To be sure, in our present status, our intellect does
not know anything with clear intuition and perfectly.[7]
Any positive extramental thing is capable of moving
the intellect to conceive that thing confusedly or to
conceive it distinctly. I call a concept confused, when
the intellect does not distinguish one thing from the
other. Socrates moves the intellect to the apprehension of the man, but by that the intellect does not distinguish nor know Socrates as distinct from Plato.
Again, a positive external thing may move the intellect
to conceive it in other than a confused way and so I say
that this Socrates is a man.[8]

It is possible to have intuitive knowledge, both sensitive and intellectual, of a thing which does not exist.
Every absolute thing, distinct in place and subject from
another absolute thing, can exist by divine power without that thing. The intuitive vision, however, both
sensitive and intellectual, is an absolute thing distinct
in place and subject from the object, as when intuitively I see a star in the sky. This intuitive vision,
whether sensitive or intellectual, is an absolute thing
distinct in place and subject from the seen object;
therefore, vision can remain after, say, the star has
been destroyed.[9] I assert, then, that there can be by
the power of God intuitive knowledge concerning a
non-existent object. Sight is a quality absolutely dis-

[5] *Sent.* II, qu. 15, E.
[6] *Sent.,* Prol., qu. 1, E.
[7] *Sent.,* Prol., qu. 1, V. V.
[8] *Sent.* I, dist. 2, qu. 7, F.
[9] *Sent.,* Prol., qu. 1, H. H.

tinct from the object: therefore, it can exist in the absence of an object.[10]

It is manifest also, that our intellect, in our present state, does not know merely sensory things, but particularly and intuitively knows some intelligible things too, which by no means are objects of the senses. To these belong acts of intellect, acts of will, pleasure, sorrow, and the like, which one can experience as internal without their being sensory or objects of the senses.[11] Contingent truths with reference to these purely intelligible facts are known to us by the intellect with greater certainty and evidence than any other contingent truths. This is manifest to us both by experience and by Saint Augustine, who in his book on the Trinity, first chapter, argues at great length that anybody could doubt the sensuous experiences, but not such experiences as these: I know I am living; I know I want to be happy; and I know that I do not want to err.[12]

As soon as the senses apprehend sensible objects, the intellect has an intuitive cognition of them.[13] The intellect proceeds from potentiality to act, and so there is no one who by apprehending any kind of singular thing, would not, or could not, understand instantly the most general concept.[14] Any thing can be known either abstractly or intuitively.[15] Abstract knowledge can be taken in two ways. One way refers to some thing abstracted from many singular objects. In this sense abstract knowledge is nothing else than the

[10] *Quodlib.*, qu. 6.
[11] *Sent.*, Prol., qu. 1, H. H.
[12] *Sent.*, Prol., qu. 1, K. K.
[13] *Sent.* II, qu. 18, P.
[14] *Sent.* I, dist. 3, qu. 5, B. B.
[15] *Sent.* I, dist. 3, qu. 2, E.

knowledge of some universal which is abstracted from
many things. In the other sense, abstract knowledge
is taken as what it abstracts from the existence and
non-existence and from other conditions which happen contingently to the thing or are predicated of it.[16]

Among acts of intellect there are two kinds. One of
them is the apprehensive, used with reference to anything which can terminate the act of intellectual potency, whether it be something complex or simple. For
we apprehend not only simple things but propositions
and demonstrations too, both necessary and possible
ones, and we apprehend generally everything which
may be considered by intellectual potency. The other
act may be called judicative, whereby the intellect not
only apprehends the object, but also gives an assent or
dissent. This act is related only to complex things,
because we do not assent intellectually except to what
we think to be true and do not dissent from something
unless we estimate it to be false.[17] The intellect by
apprehending a singular object produces a knowledge
in itself, which is of that singular thing only. This
knowledge is a state of the soul, capable of standing
for that thing. Therefore, as the word substitutes by
agreement for the thing, so the intention, too, substitutes by its nature for the thing to which it belongs in-
dependently of any verbal contrivance.[18]

An entity in the soul meant to signify something is
called the intention of the soul. This subsisting something in the soul which is a sign of the thing out of
which mental propositions are composed, is called sometimes the intention of the soul, sometimes the concept

[16] *Sent.,* Prol., qu. 1, Z.
[17] *Sent.,* Prol., qu. 1, O.
[18] *Summa tot. log.* I, 12, f. 6, r. A.

of the soul, sometimes the passion of the soul, sometimes a likeness of the thing.[19] It is sufficient that the
intention be something in the soul, a sign naturally significatory of something for which it can stand, something which may be the part of a mental proposition.
The intention is twofold: first, it is the sign of something not itself a sign. This is called the first intention. In a wide sense, it is any intentional sign subsisting in the soul, which does not directly signify intentions or signs. In this sense, mental verbs, mental
syncategoremata, adverbs, conjunctions, and such other
things may be called first intentions. In a strict sense,
however, the first intention is to be understood as a
mental name meant to stand for its signified object.
The second intention, on the other hand, is that which
is a sign of such first intentions, e. g., genus, species,
and such others.[20] The first intention is called a thing
which exists really, the second intention, on the other
hand, is called something in the soul which is applicable
to the things and is predicable of the names of things
when they do not stand in personal supposition but in a
simple one like: genus, species. The logician's task is
to determine precisely that in a proposition, say "man
is a species," the subject stands for a common something and not for some signified object. Whether that
common something is real or not real, concerns not
him but the metaphysician.[21] The logician, who does
not treat of man nor have to define man, has the task
of teaching how the other sciences which treat of man
have to define him.[22] The logician principally has to
consider the distinction between the names of first and

19 *Expos. aur.,* Perierm., Proem.
20 *Summa tot. log.* I, 12, f. 6, r. B.
21 *Sent.* I, dist. 23, qu. 1, D and J.
22 *Summa tot. log.* I, C. 26, f. 10, r. B.

second intention. And precisely herein lies the difference between the two, that the names of the first intention are those which when they substitute personally, stand precisely for things, leaving out of question their predicability of things; whereas names of the second intention stand for various modes which are predicable of things.[23] Concerning this point, I say that the act by which the intellect understands an object outside the soul is called direct, and the act by which this direct act itself is understood is called reflex.[24]

The universals and second intentions are caused naturally by the knowledge of simple terms without any activity of the intellect and the will. They come about in this manner: first, I apprehend in particular some singular objects intuitively or abstractly. This is caused by the object or by a predisposition from a former act. This act consummated, presently, if there is no obstacle, another act follows naturally, distinct from the first and terminating in something of the same kind of logical reality[24a] as was seen before in the psychological reality.[24b] This second act produces the universals and second intentions.[25] Something not there before is left behind in the imaginative faculty mediated by the intuitive cognition of particular sensation;[26] yet this is not the object of the act, but some kind of a predisposition inclined to imagine the previously sensed object.[27] I am certain that I perceive a stone in virtue of the sight of the stone and in virtue of primary vision.

[23] *Sent.* I, dist. 23, qu. 1, D. and J.
[24] *Quodlib.* II, qu. 12.
[24a] In the original, "esse objectivum."
[24b] In the original, "esse subjectivum."
[25] *Sent.* II, qu. 25, P.
[26] *Sent.* II, qu. 15, C.
[27] *Sent.* II, qu. 17, S.

I am certain that I understand by experience because I see the image of the stone. The certainty of understanding the stone, however, comes by reasoning from effect to cause. I know fire by smoke when I see smoke alone, because I have on other occasions seen smoke caused by the presence of fire. In the same manner, I know the stone because on other occasions I have perceived intellectually the production of such an image in me.[28]

Every universal is one singular thing and is universal only by the signification of many things. The universal is one and a single intention of the soul meant to be predicated of many things; in so far, however, as it is a single form subsisting really in the intellect, it is called singular.[29]

The universal is twofold: natural and conventional. The first is a natural sign predicable of many things, as smoke naturally signifies fire, and a groan the pain of the sick man, and laughter a certain interior joy. Such a universal is nothing else than such an intention of the soul that no substance outside of the soul, nor any accident outside of the soul, is a counterpart of it. The conventional universal is one by voluntary institution. Such is the spoken word, which is an actual quality, numerically one, and universal because of its being a voluntarily instituted sign for the signification of many things. Therefore, as the word is called common, the same also may be called universal, adding that this is not by the nature of the thing but only by the agreement of users.[30] Of a universal that is such by discretion, I do not speak, but I do speak of that

[28] *Quodlib.* I, qu. 14.
[29] *Summa tot. log.* I, 1, c. 14.
[30] *Summa tot. log.* I, 14, f. 6, v. B.

one which has whatever is universal in it by its very
nature.[31]

I am inquiring, now, whether this universal and uni-
vocally common entity is something real from the part
of the thing which is outside of the soul. All whom I
meet agree by saying that the entity which is somehow
universal is really in the individual, although some say
that it is distinguished really, others that it is distinguished only formally, and some that it is not distinguished at all according to the nature of the thing, but
only according to reason or by the consideration of the
intellect. All these opinions coincide in that the universals are allowed to exist somehow from the side of
the thing, so that their universality is held to be really
present in the singular objects themselves.[32]

This latter opinion is simply false and absurd.
Against it this is my case. There is no unitary, un-
varied or simple thing in a multiplicity of singular
things nor in any kind of created individuals, together
and at the same time. If such a thing were allowed,
it would be numerically one; therefore, it would not
be in many singular objects nor would it be of their
essence. But the singular and the universal thing are
by themselves two things, really distinct and equally
simple; therefore, if the singular thing is numerically
one, the universal thing will be numerically one also,
and one does not include a greater plurality intrinsic
to things than does the other.

If it is objected that the universal thing is really
communicable to many things and is really in many,
and, therefore, although it does not include intrinsically a greater plurality of things, nevertheless, it is

[31] *Summa tot. log.,* I, 22, f. 9, v. A.
[32] *Sent.* I, dist. 2, qu. 7, F.

not one numerically as the singular thing, I retort by asking how it is communicated to many things and how it is in them. If it is answered that the universal is communicated to many things without any variation and multiplication of its own, remaining really distinct from things, still such communicability or existence in a plurality would not exclude a numerical unity. Any thing making an arithmetical connection or conjunction with an other thing is either numerically one thing or numerically many things; but if we accept such a universal thing, this would truly make an arithmetical connection as with the singular object; therefore, it will be either numerically one thing, or numerically many things. But the universal is not many things, numerically; consequently, it is numerically one.

To the rejoinder that the universal thing is of the essence of Socrates and not the total essence of Socrates, because in that case the universal thing would not differ from Socrates, and that, therefore, the universal thing is an essential part of Socrates, I reply that this would result in many absurdities. It would follow therefrom that in any singular object there would be just as many really distinct things, as there are universals predicable in a univocal manner of that thing.

Besides, all external things belonging under the genus of substance may be subject to contrary statements; therefore, if there were some universal substance, it actually would be susceptible of contrary statements. But no universal can be subject to contrary statements; hence, there is no universal which would be a real thing under the heading of substance.[33]

If "humanity" were different from the particular individuals and a part of their essence, one and the same

[33] *Sent.* I, dist. 2, qu. 4, A.

invariable thing would be in many individuals, and so this same numerically one and invariable thing would be at different places, which is false. In the same way, that same invariable thing would, say, be condemned in Judas and saved in Christ and, hence, there would be something condemned and miserable in Christ, which is absurd. In much the same manner, God could not, then, annihilate an individual without destroying all the individuals of the same genus.[34]

To conclude, I say that there is no such a thing as a universal, intrinsically present in the things to which it is common.[35] No universal, except that which is such by voluntary agreement, is existent in any way outside of the soul, but everything which can be predicated of many things, is by its nature in the mind either psychologically or logically. Nothing of that sort is of the essence or quiddity of any substance.[36]

It seems to some, nevertheless, that the universal is somehow outside of the soul and present in individuals not as distinct from them really, but yet formally. Accordingly, they say that there is in Socrates a human nature which is contracted to Socrates by an individual differentia, being distinguished not really but formally from that nature. Hence, there are no two things together, yet one is not the other formally.[37] This is the opinion, as I understand, of the Subtle Doctor,[38] who excelled others in incisiveness of judgment. In the view of this doctor, there is besides the numerical unity another real unity less than the numerical unity. This

[34] *Summa tot. log.* II, 2, f. 25, v. B.
[35] *Sent.* I, dist. 2, qu. 4, D.
[36] *Sent.* I, dist. 2, qu. 8, Q.
[37] *Summa tot. log.* I, 16, f. 7, r. B.
[38] Alluding to John Duns Scotus (c. 1270-1308) the "doctor subtilis" of the Middle Ages and to his doctrine of "haecceitas" or "thisness."

entity is neither the matter nor the form nor their composite, inasmuch as every one of these is the nature, but it is the ultimate reality of being.

Against this opinion one can argue in a double manner: first, by saying that it is impossible to admit that in created things any thing differs formally without being distinguished really. Secondly, granting this distinction, the aforesaid view is still untrue. If nature were common in that manner, it follows that there would be just as many species and genera as there are individuals. Therefore, it is not to be imagined that in Socrates there is a humanity or human nature distinct in some way from Socrates, to which an individual differentia is to be added, thereby contracting that nature. Contrarily, whatever imaginable substantial thing exists in Socrates is either the particular matter or the particular form, or something composed of these. Therefore, all essence and quiddity and whatever belongs to the substance, if it is real outside of the soul, is either without qualification and absolutely the matter, or the form, or a composite of the two.[39] According to the opinion which I assert as true, there is in man more than one substantial form—at least the forms of corporeity and of the intellectual soul.[40]

As to the question whether or not essence and existence of a thing are two distinct things outside of the soul, it seems to me that they are not two things; nor does the essence of existence signify something distinct from the thing.[41] Existence and essence signify one and the same thing.[42]

The entity which is predicated of many things dif-

39 *Summa tot. log.* I, 16, f. 7, v. A.
40 *Sent.* II, qu. 9, C. C.
41 *Summa tot. log.* III, 2, 27, f. 53, v. B.
42 *Quodlib.* II, qu. 7.

fering in species, is not somehow of the essence of those things of which it is predicated; but it is an intention in the soul naturally signifying all those things of which it is predicated. Therefore, the genus is not something common to many things by some intrinsic identity, but some commonalty of a sign, as one and the same sign is common to many signified objects.

What is that in the soul, however, which is such a sign? About this question there are various opinions. There is an opinion according to which it is some quality of the soul distinct really from the act of intellect, being the object of the intellect terminating the act of understanding. This quality is a real resemblance of the external thing, by which it represents the thing and which by its nature stands for it, as a word by common consent stands for things.

There is another opinion according to which that passion of the soul is a "species" of the thing representing the thing naturally and standing naturally for it in a proposition. Yet, this opinion seems to be even more irrational than the first. Such a "species" should be disallowed on the ground of superfluity.[43] Never should anything be introduced without necessity. All that can be saved by this contrivance of "species" can just as conveniently be saved without it.[44]

Another opinion may be entertained, according to which that passion of the soul is the act of intellect itself. This seems to me to be the most probable of all opinions.[45]

Some say that the first and second intentions are fictitious entities, being in the mind only logically, and

[43] *Expos. aur.,* Perierm., Proem.
[44] *Sent.* I, dist. 27, qu. 2, J and K.
[45] *Expos. aur.,* Perierm., Proem.

that they are nowhere psychologically. Against this it may be argued that such fiction would impede the understanding of the thing; hence, it is not to be admitted for the sake of the cognition. Besides, there is no need for such a fiction in order to form the subject and predicate into a universal proposition, because an act of intellect takes care of that. Therefore, I say that both first and second intentions are veritable acts of intellect, because whatever is saved by the fiction can be saved by such an act. By the fact, indeed, that the act is a likeness of the subject, it can signify and stand for the things outside, it can be subject and predicate in a proposition, can be genus and species, just as well as a fiction can.[46]

These statements make it clear that both the first and second intentions are, in truth, real entities and real qualities psychologically subsisting in the soul.[47]

There may be entertained another opinion, according to which nothing is universal by its nature, but only by agreement. This opinion does not seem to be true, because in that case nothing would be by its nature species or genus.[48]

In order to have abstract knowledge, one must of necessity first allow something besides the object and the intellect. Something is deposited back in the imaginative faculty through the medium of the intuitive cognition of a particular sense which was not there before; otherwise the imagination in the absence of a sensible thing could not activate itself with reference to it.[49]

[46] *Sent.* II, qu. 15, Q.

[47] *Sent.* IV, qu. 19. To prevent misunderstanding we have to interpret Ockham as saying here that the second intention or the universal as an *act* of intellect exists psychologically in the soul while as *content* it exists only logically.

[48] *Sent.* I, dist. 2, qu. 8, E.

[49] *Sent.* II, qu. 15, Q.

Our intellect first understands some singular real existent intuitively, and after having understood it, the
same intellect may construct something resembling the
previously understood thing. This fictitious something,
however, cannot have a psychological, but only logical,
being.[50]   Simulacra, phantasms, idols, and images are
not something really distinguished from the things outside, but they indicate the thing itself in so far as it
terminates the act of the interior sense in the absence
of the sensible thing.[51]   Genera and differentiae and
other universals have no ideas, unless it be granted that
the universals are things existing psychologically in the
soul and common to external things only by predication.[52]   The universal is not some real thing having a
psychological being in the soul or outside of the soul.[53]
It has only a logical being in the soul and is a sort of
fiction having the same sort of existence in the logical
realm as the external thing has in the ontological[54]
realm.   Figments have no psychological being in the
soul, because then they would really be things, and,
thus, a chimera and a centaur[55] and the like would all
be real things.   There are, then, certain entities which
have only logical being.   In the same way, propositions,
syllogisms, and such other things as logic treats, have
no psychological being, but have a logical being only:
so their being is their being understood.[56]   In the same
way almost all distinguish the second intentions from

50 *Sent.* I, dist. 13, qu. 1, J.

51 *Sent.* II, qu. 17, S.

52 *Sent.* I, dist. 35, qu. 5, G.

53 The term of the original "esse subjectivum" implies both
intra-mental and extra-mental existentiality.

54 In the original: "in esse subjectivo."

55 In the original: "hircocervus."

56 In the original: "ita quod eorum esse est eorum cognosci."

the first intentions, by not calling the second intentions real qualities of the soul. Therefore, as they do not exist really, they can exist only logically in the soul.[57]

The term "knowing" (scientia) or "concept" does not signify a quality in the soul only, but it signifies also the coexistence of the object, and the conformity of the object to the "knowing" (scientia) of the object. I mean not a simple but a complex object, which has a mode of existence whereby the intellect gives assent to it.[58] The universal is not such a "fiction" as it has nothing similar corresponding to it in the ontological[59] realm; it is not a figment like a chimera or something of that sort. That thing can be called a universal which is an exemplar related without any difference to all external single things and which because of that similitude in the logical realm can stand for the external things.[60]

In virtue of the connotation of the term we should not concede that Socrates and Plato concur in some thing or things, but that they concur *by means* of some things, because they concur *through themselves*. Hence, when it is said that Socrates and Plato coincide in "man," I would say that "man" may substitute either in a simple or a direct way.[61] As to the simple, it may be admitted, because that would mean nothing else than that "man" is a common something predicable of Socrates and Plato. On the other hand, the notion that "man" substitutes directly for anything is simply false, because Socrates and Plato do not coincide in any common "man" nor in any other thing, but they do

[57] *Sent.* I, dist. 2, qu. 8, F.
[58] *Sent.* III, qu. 4, R.
[59] In the original: "in esse subjectivo."
[60] *Sent.* I, dist. 2, qu. 8, F and E.
[61] That is, personally.

coincide by means of things, through themselves because they are men.[62]

Nevertheless we do have a science of singular things,
on the basis that terms stand for the singular things
themselves.   It is irrelevant for real science, whether
the terms of the known proposition are things outside
of the soul or only in the soul, taking it for granted
all along that they substitute and stand for the things
themselves; and, therefore, it is not necessary for a
real science to assume universal things set off from
singular objects by a real distinction.[63]

Having spoken of the terms of propositions and the
things for which they stand, something has to be said
about the term "being" and "one," which are common
to everything, whether they are things that are not signs
or things that are signs.

The term "being" corresponds to the concept common to all things of which existence can be predicated.   Yet this term is equivocal.   For when it is
taken in a significative manner, it is not predicated of
the things belonging to it according to one concept, but
according to different concepts corresponding to it.[64]
The term "one" is a variation of the term "being," because it signifies something which is also signified by
"being" but not in the same way.   At present, however,
it should suffice to point out merely the three modes
which are most frequently used by logicians, namely:
the one by number, the one by species, and the one by
genus.[65]

To continue our inquiry we come now to the things

[62] *Sent.* I, dist. 2, qu. 6, E. E.

[63] *Sent.* I, dist. 2, qu. 4, N.

[64] *Summa tot. log.,* C. 38, f. 12, v. A.

[65] *Summa tot. log.,* C. 39, f. 12, v. B.

which belong under the term "being" as its subordinates, that is, to the ten predicaments: substance, quantity, quality, relation, action, passion, place, date, position, state.[66] It may be stated that in fact there are only three highest genera: substance, quality, and relation.[67] There is another opinion which to me seems to give the view of Aristotle, be it heretic or catholic. I want to introduce it now without affirming it. At the time when I wrote about philosophy, I did not present it as my own but as one which, to my mind, comes nearest to Aristotle's exposition. This opinion, which I advance without affirming although many Catholics and theologians hold it and held it, says that no quantity is really distinguishable from substance and quality.[68]

This term "predicament" is one of second imposition or intention as is the term "genus," although the things of which it is predicated are simple elements of the first intention. The predicament taken in this sense is a simple element of a first intention signifying things which are not signs. Nevertheless, it should be noted that the predicament is an entity of reason, because it is nowhere but in the reason. It is in this sense that all propositions and consequences and mental terms are to be considered as entities of the reason, without denying that they exist truly and really also in the nature of things.[69] Aristotle in his treatise *On the Predicaments*

[66] *Summa tot. log.* C. 40, f. 13, r. A.

[67] *Sent.* I, dist. 8, qu. 2, D.

[68] *Summa tot. log.* I, 44, f. 15, v. A. This doctrine is openly subversive to the dogma of Transubstantiation according to which the substance of the bread and wine is separable from their "species," i. e., accidents, and may be substituted by the substance of the body and blood of Christ.

[69] *Summa tot. log.* I, 40, f. 13, r. B.

determined how words signify things. And ignorance of the intention of Aristotle in this book is the cause of the error on this point of many moderns, who believe that Aristotle was in this connection discussing things, while in the fact he was only concerned with words and correspondingly with intentions or concepts in the soul. The predicaments do not represent a division of things outside of the soul, for external things are not predicated of one another. Nothing can be predicated save a word or concept or some arbitrarily instituted sign. What we have here is a division of words or concepts or intentions in the soul. There is outside of the soul really no substance except the particular substance. Aristotle does not say that the ten predicaments are ten entities intrinsically present in all the rest of things, but that they are ten principles, that is, ten common intentions, which can be predicated of things under their respective domains.[70]

[70] *Expos. aur.*, Praedicam., Proem.

ON THE IDEAS OF GOD

The Christian world-view during its gradual adjustment to the Greco-Roman civilization found a solid anchorage for the restless flux of life in the philosophy of the essence of the ancients. The Platonic idea or the Aristotelian form was accepted as permanent, self-abiding foundation for the physical universe and for the dialectical and ethical operations of man. Yet these metaphysical grounds were not considered sanctioned until the essences of the Hellenes were shifted into the mind of God by a gradual process which, beginning as early as Philo of Alexandria (ca. 25 B. C.-40 A. D.), can clearly be traced in the writings of the Middle Platonists, Albinus (ca. 130 A. D.) and Atticus (ca. 176 A. D.) ; it was developed by the Neo-Platonist, Plotinus (204-270 A. D.), and attained its final and authoritative formulation with Saint Augustine (354-430). Through him the philosophy of the ideas of God became the "magna charta" of the world-process for the medievalists and their followers.

William of Ockham in the following chapter, which constitutes the fifth question of the thirty-fifth distinction in his Commentary to the First Book of the *Sentences,* attempts to assail this avowedly indefeasible anchor of his age which was considered a metaphysical guarantee for order and security. He eliminated the "universale ante rem" from the mind of God and propounded a new theory according to which God's ideas are not conditioned by His essence, conceived as an intellectual blueprint, but are entirely unconditioned and freely produced with the things themselves. In this account an idea of God is the created thing itself in so far as it is comprehended by the divine intellect. Consequently, an idea, just as any created thing, is rooted in the volitional nature of God.

Of what tremendous significance these views are for a philosophy of existence and free becoming as against a philosophy of essence based on unchangeable being and immutable patterns, may be readily seen. For that reason, we may rightly call this treatise the most revolutionary chapter of the Middle Ages.

IN the fifth place I am inquiring: Does God know all things which are not Himself by means of their ideas?

It will be argued thus: An idea is a ground of knowing. Now as there is no ground whereby God knows

the divine essence, therefore, there is no ground whereby He knows something which is not Himself.

On the contrary: God knows everything by means
of His essence, therefore, not by means of ideas. The
consequence is evident: because neither God nor the
divine essence is an idea; for, in that case just as there
are many ideas there would be a number of essences, a
thing which is impossible.

With regard to this question this will be the manner
of proceeding: first, we will have to see what is meant
by idea; second, we will have to see what is the necessity of positing ideas; third, after having examined
these points, we will treat the question itself.

As to the first article: many doctors, indeed almost
all of them, are unanimous in holding one common
view that an idea is actually[1] the divine essence and
yet differs by a distinction of reason[2] from the divine
essence. Consequently some say that God knows the
created thing not only in so far as it is actually identical
with Himself, but knows it also in so far as it is different from Himself. From this it follows that the divine
essence itself is the ground and exemplary form of
creatures, and as the form and cause and formal principle of the things exemplified, this divine essence is
the ground of knowing them. Now this ground in the
divine essence whereby His essence is the basis of
knowing things different from Himself, is nothing else
than an imitability[3] by means of which His essence can
be understood by others. We call such a ground[4] or

[1] In the original: "realiter."

[2] In the original: "ratione."

[3] I. e., quality of being imitable, a word referring to the
Platonic doctrine of imitation.

[4] In the original: "ratio."

aspect[5] in the divine essence an idea, considering that essence not in itself and absolutely—except in its virtual power and as it were in potentiality—but in so far as this essence is already known, and is the first object of the divine intellect in actual operation. And precisely through this operation does that ground have subsistence in the essence, that is, by virtue of the fact that the divine intellect considers the divine essence and comprehends it under the aspect of imitability. In this view, an idea, formally considered, is nothing else than an aspect of imitability in the divine essence itself, in so far as it is considered by the intellect.

Against this commonly held view I will show that an idea is not really identical with the divine essence. For an idea either indicates precisely the divine essence, or precisely the aspect, or a composite of the essence and aspect, because none of those writers mentions the view which says that an idea means essence and something absolute, or precisely something absolute over and above essence.

In the first case, just as there is only one essence, so there would be only one idea, and that is not held by any of them. In the second case, that aspect is either real or rational. If it is a real aspect, it could not be anything else but the fatherhood or the sonhood or the spirit-relationship;[6] but every one of these would be considered false by them. In the same manner, they would not accept a real relationship between God and the created world either. If this aspect is a rational entity we have won the case, because it is impossible

5 In the original: "respectus," a term indicating a particular consideration of reason in the analysis of some entity.

6 In the original: "spiratio," meaning the procession of the Holy Spirit from both the Father and the Son as from one single principle.

that an entity of reason would be objectively identical with a real entity. Whatever is identical really with a real entity is veritably a real thing and, consequently, not a rational entity and so on. Therefore, if an idea indicates only an aspect of reason, it is not in fact the divine essence. In the third case, the idea could not be the divine essence either. This last consequence is plain. When something is a composite or is constituted out of many things which actually differ from each other, that whole is not the same thing as any of its constituents. A composite is not really matter nor is it really form. Therefore, both of these propositions: the composite is really form, the composite is really matter, are false.

As to the second article, the assertion is made as we saw it above that it is necessary to posit ideas in God for four reasons: First, ideas are necessary for God to know things which are not Himself, perfectly, according to the ground, in so far as they are different from Himself. And we have to assume many such ideas in God, so that He could know things which are not Himself perfectly. As Saint Augustine says in his treatise on ideas, there is such a power in the ideas that without understanding them, He could not be wise, meaning in that knowledge whereby He is to know things which are not Himself. And because such a knowledge of things on the part of God is the exemplary cause of things relating a thing to Him according to essence, for that reason, as a second point, it is necessary, to save this essential relationship, to place many ideas in God because of the plurality of created things all differing by species. Thus, He has principally the singular things present in His knowledge from eternity as in an archetypal world.[7]   Third, it is necessary to posit in God, although not by virtue of the ideas, all the perfections of things also, whereby He is the proper measure of each thing.   But perfection and idea differ in God only by a distinction of reason. Fourth, it is necessary to posit ideas because of the production of things in actual existence.   God could not produce many diverse and distinct things, unless He had a knowledge of them in producing them.   But such a knowledge does not exist except by ideas.

Although some of these statements according to their tenor sound true, nevertheless according to the intention of their proponent I consider them without qualification false.   For what their proponent intends to say is that these ideas which are introduced are not identical with the created things themselves, but are to be considered as certain aspects of imitability whereby the divine essence can be imitated by the created things. But none of the aforesaid reasons provide the necessity of positing such ideas.   Therefore, it is not necessary to posit ideas such as he posits in God.   The major premise is conceded by them.   As to the minor, I will prove it in the following manner.

First, contrary to the supposition of the first argument, it is manifest that ideas in God are unnecessary because the divine intellect could know all things which are not Himself without any aspects of reason.   Further, these aspects would be derogatory to His intellect.   For if the divine intellect would understand things which are not Himself through these (aspects) so that the object itself would be the constitutive factor

[7] In the original: "mundus archetypus," a conception originating from the *Timaeus* of Plato, utilized by Philo and Plotinus and widely accepted by the medievals.

in the act of knowing, this fact would detract from His intellect. Therefore, if the divine essence alone were not a sufficient moving cause of His intellect for the understanding of all other things, it would ˙require something else, and the result would be a disparagement of His intellect. Still further, that aspect of reason either precedes the knowledge of created things, or follows the knowledge of created things. The first could not be, because according to this (alternative) since (in any case) an aspect of reason must necessarily follow some act of knowing, then such an aspect would follow that act of the divine intellect whereby He understands His own essence in an absolute manner, that is, without comparing it to something else. This possibility, however, is denied by them. The second alternative could not occur either. Partly, because the aspect then would not contribute anything toward God's distinct understanding of things which are not God, just as the effect does not contribute anything to the being of its cause which it follows; partly, because such an aspect of reason does not follow the knowing act whereby God understands His own essence, therefore, for the same reason, it does not follow the act of knowing by which He understands something that is not Himself. The reason for it would not be greater in one case than in the other.

Secondly, I show that according to the second reason it is not necessary to posit many such ideas in God. A created artificer can have a distinct notion of many things and can produce different things without any aspect of reason. So much more could the uncreated artificer know many things distinctly and produce them afterwards in actual existence without any such aspect of reason.

Thirdly, I show that such ideas need not be posited according to the third reason. If the perfection of the created thing in God and the idea are the same thing, I am asking, is that perfection in God really God Himself or is it not? If it is, then, because God is not plural, the ideas will not in reality be plural either. If not (that is, if this perfection is not God) this would be against the proponent because he states that the idea is really identical with the divine essence. In the same manner, nothing that is not God can be the proper measure of the supreme creature;[8] now because, according to this proponent, that perfection is the measure of the created thing, it would follow that the supreme creature would have no idea in God.

As to the fourth reason, it is evident by all which has been said that it is not a valid one. In order to produce something the artificer does not need any such thing as an aspect of reason.

As a consequence, my solution of this question will be arranged in a different manner. I am approaching it in this way: first, it is to be seen what is the meaning[9] of what I call idea; secondly, it is to be seen to what thing that meaning should be applied; this will clear up the first article; thirdly, it is to be seen what is the necessity of positing ideas; in the fourth place, I will draw certain conclusions; in the fifth place, I will give my answer to the problem as formulated in the question; in the sixth place, I shall raise some doubts and shall solve them.

Proceeding to my first point, it is to be known that

[8] I. e., the creature which is nearest to God without any intermediary.

[9] In the original: "quid nominis," indicating the logical essence.

an idea is not an existential thing.[10] An idea is a connotative term, or to employ another mode of speech, it is a relative term. For every idea is necessarily the "ideal" of something or the idea of an ideatum,[11] and, therefore, it does not precisely signify one single thing, but it signifies one thing and connotes something in addition, this latter being the very thing which is being signified.[12] For this reason an idea has only a logical entity[13] and may be described this way: an idea is something known, something apprehended by an effective intellectual principle, to which that agent may look in order to produce something in actual existence.

This description is apparent as to its first part from what Saint Augustine says in his LXXXIII Questions, question 43, with these words: Where shall we think these grounds are but in the very mind of the Creator, for He does not look to anything existing outside of Himself to bring about the things that He created. From this authority it is manifest that the ideas are known by the divine mind. The second part, asserting that an idea is something known by an intellectual agent is also manifest by the same authority when he says: "where shall we look for these grounds but in the very mind of the Creator?" The third part, which says that the idea is the means by the contemplation of which one is able to produce something in actual existence, is manifest from the end which the same authority had in view when he says: for He does not look to

[10] In the original: "quid rei," indicative of ontological existence.

[11] I. e., produced according to an idea, "nam omnis idea necessario est alicuius idealis vel ideati idea."

[12] For instance: Socrates is white by whiteness; white connotes the concept whiteness.

[13] In the original: "habet tantum quid nominis" is a meaning only.

anything existing outside of Himself to bring into existence the things that He created according to its pattern. This authority manifestly intends to intimate that God looks at the ideas in order to create, that is, bring things into existence according to those ideas.

This description is apparent by Seneca's 46th Letter, too, where he, after enumerating the four causes laid down by Aristotle, speaks in this way: to these four a fifth one may be added, that is, the exemplary cause of Plato called by him idea. To this the artificer looks with a view of bringing whatever is deficient into existence. For it does not matter whether the exemplar to which the eye looks is outside or inside, when the artificer conceives. From this authority it is manifest that ideas are certain known exemplars, and that their beholder, by looking up to them may produce something in actual existence.

Proceeding to my second point, I say that this description of the idea is not applicable to the divine essence itself, nor to any aspect of reason, but to the created thing itself.

The first part is obvious. First, because according to all, there are many ideas. In that sense, says Augustine, in his above treatise that a different ground underlies the creation of man and a different one the creation of a horse, and he takes the (term), "ground,"[14] for idea. But the divine essence is one, and not to be made plural by any means; therefore, it is not itself an idea. But it may be answered that although the essence itself cannot be really plural, yet, in so far as it can be compared to the diverse created things, it can be now one, now another idea. And in this way we may have many ideas differing from each

[14] In the original: "ratione."

other not in actuality[15] but by virtue of reason[16] only. Such and similar objections, however, were sufficiently refuted before when we said that it is impossible to admit things actually self-identical and yet differing from each other by virtue of reason. In the same manner, if the divine essence were in reality many ideas, my reply is: either the idea is precisely the divine essence or it is the divine essence and something else in addition, that is, an aspect of reason as they say. In the first case, the divine essence is many divine essences, if there are many ideas. In the second case, the divine essence is not an idea.

Second, I show that the divine essence is not an idea. For in my inquiry the ideas are in the divine mind either psychologically[17] or logically.[18] They are not psychological entities in it which is openly false. Consequently, ideas are in the divine mind only logically. However, the divine essence does not exist logically only, therefore, it is not an idea.

The second part which states that the aspect of reason is not idea, will be proved thus. This aspect is either an actual entity[19] or an entity of reason.[20] It cannot be an actual entity because according to the afore-mentioned view God has no real relation to the created thing. It cannot be an entity of reason either.

[15] In the original: "realiter."

[16] In the original: "ratione."

[17] In the original: "subjective"; "Esse subjectivum" stands for ontological existence, mental or extramental and it indicates subject, i. e., subjective or substantial being.

[18] In the original: "objective"; "Esse objectivum" stands for logical existence, that is, for something which exists only as known or understood by the intellect.

[19] In the original: "respectus realis."

[20] In the original: "respectus rationis."

On the one hand, because there is no such relation of God to the created world which could be indicated by the name of idea; on the other, because such an aspect cannot be the exemplar of the created thing just as an entity of reason cannot be the exemplar of an actual entity.

The third part, stating that the created thing itself is the idea, is proved in the following manner. First, it is the created thing to which all the parts of the above mentioned description can be applied. For the created thing is something understood by an active intellect, and God looks to it in order to produce rationally. For no matter how much God might know His essence, if He did not know his creature to be produced, He would produce ignorantly and not rationally and consequently not by an idea. Therefore, He really looks to the creature and by looking to it He can produce. Further, precisely that thing is a true idea and exemplar by the foreknowledge of which the one knowing can rationally produce even when everything else is, to suppose the impossible, not foreknown and without the foreknowledge of which even if everything else would be known, he cannot rationally produce. In other words, assuming by way of impossibility that God would know the producible created thing and would not know His own essence, if He had the power of producing, He could really produce rationally. On the other hand, no matter how much God knew His essence, unless He knew the created thing, He could not be said to produce rationally no matter how many things He would produce. Therefore, the created thing itself is the idea.

Further, ideas should be posited proportionately in

the created and uncreated artificer. But, if the created
artificer knew precisely the work of art to be produced,
he would just as truly act by means of an exemplar
and consequently by an idea, when as he knew one
thing the likeness of which he had to produce. For
such a created artificer, then, the producible thing itself would be truly the idea and exemplar, because
ideas and exemplars are identified by authors. Therefore, when God foreknows the producible created
thing itself, the created thing is veritably the idea.

This will be manifest by the following allusion.[21]
Plato, whose view is held by Saint Augustine, desig-
nates the ideas of man with such names as "man," or
the "quiddity of man," or the "universal man." This
same view is attributed to Plato by the Philosopher
when he says that Plato accepts the ideas as certain
things, distinct from each other by a real distinction,
just as the produced objects themselves are distinguished by their species. The intention of Plato, then,
was not to say that the divine essence is the idea, but
that there are certain other things known by God which
are exemplars and to which God looks in producing.
But what else among all the things known could the
theologian accept for the idea more conveniently than
the created thing itself. This will be further elucidated
in the solution of doubts. Therefore, we may proceed
to the conclusion.[22]

It is clear from the foregoing what an idea is. We
have seen that it is nothing else than something known
to which the agent looks while producing, so that he
may produce something similar or produce the same

[21] In the original: "per signum," that is, the following is not
given by demonstrative knowledge but by reference to authority.

[22] That is, that the created thing is the idea.

thing in actual existence. An example would be a house which could be truly the idea and exemplar of another house. The artificer, keeping that house before his eyes, is thereby in the position to make something similar to it. Now, in the same manner, if the same house in particular were foreknown by the artificer, and by virtue of it he produced the same house in actual existence, this house would be its own idea. For that reason the idea brings along the created thing directly and itself as well, indirectly. Besides this, it implies the divine cognition or knower indirectly. And therefore it is the created thing itself of which the term idea is predicable; and it should not be predicated of the knowing agent or of the cognition, because neither the cognition nor the knower is the idea or exemplar.

Proceeding to my third point, I say (first) that we do not have to admit ideas as grounds of knowing the created things themselves as something different from them. The reason is that besides the divine essence, which is identical in every way with the divine knowledge, there are no other things that could be the grounds of knowing the creation, and, therefore, there are not many grounds to know the created things.

This is evident if we consider what we mean by the ground of knowing the created thing. This ground is either that which somehow is connected with the knowledge of the created thing, as something moving effectively the divine intellect to the knowledge of the created things; or the cognition itself whereby the created thing is known; or something that receives, as it were, the knowledge itself of the created thing; or something necessarily required for the knowledge of the created things.

The first could not be the case, because the knowledge of the created things, owing to the common participation of the divine essence by the three persons, cannot be caused at all. It is something, which cannot be produced either, and consequently the divine intellect cannot be moved by anything at all. It would be contradictory to its very being to be moved by anything, just as it is contradictory to the divine cognition to be made or created by any one.

Neither could the second possibility be the case, because the cognition of God is the same with regard to all created things and it cannot be made plural at all. Plurality precisely is in the things known, not in the cognition by any means, neither according to reality nor according to reason, and consequently, because in the opinion of all there are many ideas, they are in no manner grounds of knowing, taking ground as a way of knowing in the above manner.

The third possibility could not be true either. The divine intellect is not receptive in knowing at all; the divine intellect is the divine cognition itself formally and entirely, considered in itself.[23] In the same manner, the divine intellect cannot be made plural in any way, therefore, the divine intellect in no way partakes of an idea.

Nor can the fourth possibility be the case. If such things (supposedly required for the knowledge of the created things) were distinguished from the created world, they would still be entities of reason. For, according to all, outside of God and the created things, no other real being can be assumed. But no more is it necessary to assume entities of reason for the knowledge of actual entities than are actual things required

[23] In the original: "sed est (intellectus divinus) ipsamet cognitio formaliter et omnibus modis a parte rei."

for the knowledge of entities of reason. In fact, it would be more fitting to assume that actual entities should be grounds of knowing entities of reason than vice versa.

Secondly, I say that we ought not to assume ideas as resemblances representing the created world to the divine intellect. Such resemblances could not be the divine essence, because that is not to be made plural by any means. It is not necessary either, that these resemblances be entities of reason, because no such things are required either to produce or to know. Therefore, I say that we have to assume ideas precisely in order to have them as some exemplars, to which the divine intellect looks to produce the created things. The reason for this is that according to Saint Augustine in his aforesaid passage, precisely because God operates rationally, do we have to assume ideas in Him. Therefore, says Saint Augustine, who would dare to say that God created everything irrationally, as if he would say that for a rational agent not only productive and operative power is required but an exemplar too, to which the agent would look in operation. But the ideas are not the productive or causative power of the producer; therefore, they are exemplars and we must assume them so that they would function as exemplars.

Proceeding to my fourth point we have to know that from the points so far discussed, many conclusions follow, concerning which various questions will be raised. First, it follows that ideas are not in God psychologically and actually but are in Him only logically, as something known by Him, because the ideas are the things themselves which are producible by God. The second conclusion is that all producible things have distinct ideas, just as the things themselves are dis-

tinct among themselves.   Another conclusion which
follows is that we have distinct ideas both of matter
and of form, and generally of all essential and integral
parts.   Fourthly, it follows that ideas primarily are of
singular things and not of species; therefore, only
singular things are producible in the external world
and no other things.   In the fifth place, it follows that
there are no ideas of genera and differentiae and other
universals, unless we take the position that universals
are something existing psychologically[24] in the soul
and are common to things outside only by predication.
In the sixth place, it follows that there are no ideas of
negations, privations, evil and sin, and similar things
which are not things distinct from other things.   In
the seventh place, it follows that God has an infinite
number of ideas, as there are infinitely many things
which can be produced by Him.

On the basis of the preceding I (will come to my
fifth point, and) answer the form of the question which
inquires whether God knows all things which are not
Himself through the intermediacy of the ideas of them.

The "through" (in the preceding sentence) may
mean the factor of a motive cause as when we say that
the soul understands "through" a habit as by a motive
or effective cause; or it (i. e., the "through") may
mean the factor of an intellectual potency, as when we
say that man understands "through" intellect; or it may
mean the factor of an intermediary object, as when
we say that we know God in this life "through" a certain concept unique to Him; or it may mean the factor
of the terminating object, as when we say that we

[24] In the original: "subjective," meaning that in this case
ideas were existential entities in God.

shall see God "through" His essence, because the very divine essence in itself will be seen.

The first three modes will not give the way according to which God knows through ideas the things different from Himself. Ideas do not move the divine intellect; neither are they the intellect itself; nor are they some intermediary object between God and the other things known by Himself. But the fourth mode can be accepted, because the very things known by Him that are different from God are the ideas.

Proceeding to my sixth point, I raise some doubts against what was said in the foregoing. First, it seems that the ideas are actually and psychologically in God, which fact may be proved in several ways. One way would be to say that whatsoever is eternal exists actually in God, because otherwise something else than God would be eternal. But ideas are eternal according to Saint Augustine, who in the LXXXIII Questions, question 46 says: "ideas are certain principal forms, or fixed and unchangeable grounds of things, which, themselves, are not formed and for that reason are eternal and thus always self-identical." In the same way he adds next, "that if these grounds of all things to be created and already created are contained in the divine mind, and if nothing but eternal and unchangeable can exist in the divine mind, and if further, these principal grounds of things are the ideas of Plato, they are not only ideas, but they are true also because they are eternal and true and remain unchangeable." From this authority it is manifest that the ideas are principal forms and that they are true and eternal. But all this cannot be attributed except to such things as are in God actually. Another way of stating the same doubt is this: those things, by the vision of which the soul finds its beatitude, are actually and psychologically in God. But such are the ideas according to Saint Augustine, who in the above-mentioned treatise says that the soul finds its complete happiness by the vision of ideas.

The second doubt is the following: it does not seem that the created things themselves are the ideas. Those things that cannot be looked at except by a saintly soul could not be the created things, because those things can be seen as well by a non-saintly as a saintly soul. But according to Augustine, the ideas can be beheld by only a saintly soul, when he says in the above mentioned treatise that not every and any rational soul is capable of that vision but only such as is saintly and pure. In that place he asserts that the eye must be similar to that delicate vision of the ideas and that the soul must possess pure, sane, sincere, serene eyes to see with such eyes as are attuned to the things which she intends to see. Further, nothing can be the exemplar of itself, for between the exemplar and the thing to be exemplified there is a distinction. Therefore, the thing itself, which is distinct, is not the idea. Again, if the created thing itself were the idea, it would follow that the idea would in no other way be eternal than a stone which exists outside of the mind, and, as a consequence, the idea would not be eternal, which is against the preceding view of Saint Augustine and Seneca. It was said there that God has within Himself the exemplars of all things, and He, being full of these forms, embraces with His mind the numbers and the modes of all those things which are to be produced. These forms are called by Plato ideas, immortal, immobile, and unproducible, but the created things are mortal, changeable, and producible. Moreover, ideas according to them neither originate nor perish, but everything that can originate and perish is said to be in the process of formation, and everything that originates also perishes according to Augustine as stated in the preceding. But it is impossible that one and the same thing would originate and would not originate, would perish and would not perish. Therefore, the created things which originate and perish are not ideas because ideas neither originate nor perish.

The third doubt is this: It does not seem that ideas are only of particular things, because Plato introduced the ideas of species and not of particular objects. But Saint Augustine approves the doctrine of Plato; therefore, ideas are not primarily of particular objects.

The fourth doubt is this: besides those ideas which are introduced as the particular things, some other ideas are to be assumed also. God must surely be of as great efficiency in producing as any created artificer. But the created artificer having the universal knowledge of a house, can produce a particular house by an idea, and, consequently, the particular house itself is not the idea, but something else than the particular house. Therefore, because God does not have the knowledge of particular things only, but of universals also; not only the particular things will be ideas for Him, but the universals themselves as well, for He looks to the universals, while producing, just as much as to the particulars.

To the first of these difficulties I answer that the ideas are not in God actually and psychologically, but logically only, just as all created things were in God from eternity, because God knew them from eternity. And that is the reason why we cannot find one single passage in Augustine where he places the ideas anywhere but in the divine intelligence; they are not put in the essence, indicating thereby that ideas are not in God except in so far as they are known, and not as if they exist there as actual entities. For that reason, he says that we should not consider these ideas anywhere but in the mind of the Creator; and in the referred to statement he said that they are contained in the divine intelligence.

In answer to the authority of Augustine, I say that eternal may be taken in a twofold manner. In one way, in the proper sense of the word, we may take it for that which truly and strictly and really exists actually as eternal. In the other way, for that which is eternally, immutably understood or known, and this usage employs the word eternal in an improper sense by extension of the meaning. In the first manner, in my view, the ideas are not eternal, but God alone is eternal in this way. In the second manner, ideas are eternal, that is, they are eternally and immutably known. And in this sense Saint Augustine and other saints and philosophers speak when they say that the ideas are eternal and immortal and not producible, meaning that they are eternally, immortally, immutably, unproducibly understood. Such expressions have only the purpose of suggesting the difference between the divine mind, and the mind of any created artificer, because the ideas are eternal in the divine mind; that is, they are eternally and unchangeably understood by Him. And when it is said that created things are not eternal, I answer that the created things are not eternal, taking eternal in the first sense; but taking it in the second sense it is not unfitting to attribute eternity to them, because this is the same thing as to say that the created things are eternally understood. However, be-

cause this name idea, by virtue of its usage, connotes
the cognition whereby we know, while the created
things, denoted by the name of stone or of man and so
on, do not have such usage; for that reason, the saints
frequently concede that the ideas are eternal rather
than that the created things are. Yet, whether we say
the one or the other, we talk improperly and loosely
of the eternal.

But it may be objected that according to the same
authority the ideas are true because they are eternal
and, therefore, they were true from eternity and were
not merely understood. Again, according to the same
authority, the ideas are principal forms, or the fixed
grounds of things, etc. From this authority it will be
inferred, that the notion of "principal" involves the
notion of less principal; therefore, there are, besides
the ideas, some other forms, or grounds, not principal
ones. Consequently, there are some things which are
not ideas; therefore, not every thing is an idea.

To the first of these objections my answer is: Saint
Augustine expresses himself in an improper sense
when he says that the ideas are true. What he means
properly is that the ideas are understood as true. This
explains why, according to some, the created things
existed from eternity in the potentiality of God but
not in His nature, so that in their view the created
things existed and did not exist. Such statements cannot be accepted as the words seem to suggest because
that would involve a contradiction. They are to be
understood in this way: the created things existed in
the potentiality of God, that is, it was possible for
God, who existed from eternity to produce them, but
the existence of these things simply was not an actual
one. And so I say that when Augustine makes the re-

mark that the ideas are true, he is to be interpreted in
this sense: they are understood as true from eternity
by God, who truly is from eternity.   And if it would
be replied that in this manner it may be conceded that
man truly existed from eternity, because he is truly
understood from eternity, etc., my answer is: if the
mode of expression adopted by the saints were understood in this manner, one meaning may be conceded
just as much as the other.   However, the saints do
not think in the way just mentioned, the reason for
which was pointed out before.

To the second objection, I say: it is not the intention
of Saint Augustine to assume in addition to the ideas
some other things less fundamental which are not ideas.
His reason for naming the ideas principal forms is
that the things were by nature and duration ideas before they were actually existing outside of God, and
because as ideas they are necessarily such, while as
actual existents they are not necessary, but contingent.   Therefore, they are necessarily understood by
God, and thus are necessarily ideas, but are not necessarily existing in the nature of things.

Nevertheless, there may arise here a verbal difficulty: namely, whether the idea is to be called idea
with regard to what is already ideated or what can be
ideated; that is, whether an idea should precisely be
named such when God actually produces according to
it, or whether it should be named so even when He
does not produce according to it although He could
do so.   In answer to this difficulty it may be said that
it is more customary in the language of the saints to
use the word idea even in the case when God does not
actually produce according to it.   And for that reason,

things were ideas from eternity, but they were not actual existents from eternity.

But it may be objected that this is impossible because of the fact that according to the foregoing view of Seneca, the idea is the fifth cause in addition to the four causes which were laid down by Aristotle. But nothing can be the cause of itself; therefore, the thing which was originally idea, is not afterwards the ideated or caused thing. Further, when the saints attribute a certain kind of causality to the idea, they attribute the same to the exemplar also, and for that reason the idea is called exemplary cause. To this I answer, that properly speaking there is no cause beyond the four causes laid down by Aristotle. Therefore, the idea or exemplar properly speaking is not a cause. However, if we want to apply the name "cause" to everything the knowledge of which is presupposed in the production of something, the idea or exemplar may be a cause. And in this sense Seneca and other saints speak about cause, using the word in an extended sense. And accordingly, it is not contradictory that the idea be its own cause, as it is not contradictory that the thing to be produced is necessarily to be foreknown. If one uses the word in this sense, to be a cause means nothing else than to be foreknown, so that the thing would come into existence according to its own self; or that something similar would come into existence which belongs to its own idea and not to some other idea also producible. And it is in this sense that Saint Augustine says that the particular objects are caused by means of their own grounds. To the second point I say that the vision of the ideas adds only certain accidental happiness to beatitude, because it is the beatifying vision which is the great perfection of the rational soul.

To the second doubt, on the basis of the foregoing, I say that the creatures themselves are the ideas insofar as they are understood by God.

To the first part of this doubt, I am making the following objection: the word intuit is taken sometimes strictly for the intuitive act, sometimes widely for certain and evident knowledge or at least for true knowledge. In the first manner, the non-saintly soul may intuit the ideas, at least some of the ideas. Some other ideas only a saintly soul can intuit, such as the ideas of separated and blessed substances which can be intuited only by a saintly and blessed soul. To intuit the ideas in the second manner means to understand some truths about them with certain knowledge. And in this manner the non-saintly soul may intuit the ideas with regard to certain truths, although he may not intuit the ideas with regard to other truths which are open to the saintly soul. And this conception refers to this earthly path just as well as to our heavenly home, since many things can be known by the saints which cannot be known by others because of defect in practice and experience. And this is perhaps what Saint Augustine means. I say, then, that Saint Augustine speaks either about the blessed saintly soul which can know many truths about the ideas hidden from the non-saintly soul, that is, the not blessed soul; or that he means that the saintly soul may possess many truths about the ideas in this life, either by divine illumination or by practice and experience, which cannot be possessed by the non-saintly soul and especially by an infidel soul. Thus, the saintly soul knows that all ideas are in the divine mind, that is, that they are known eternally. He also knows that all things have ideas in God; that is, that God is the efficient cause of everything; and similar truths which, or many of which, are not known by the infidels. And if it will be objected that Saint Augustine in the afore-mentioned authoritative passage calls the ideas things, but maintains that creatures are not ideas since they were not things from eternity, I reply that in reality the converse difficulty appears. If the ideas are things, they are many things, but in God there are only three things; consequently, if ideas are actually and psychologically in God, there are not more than three ideas, which view is manifestly false. For Saint Augustine says that the particular things are created by means of their own grounds.

As to the second part of this doubt, it is apparent that something can be the exemplar of itself. Just as an existential house which is known can be the exemplar of another house to be made, because it precisely is the thing to which the artificer looks to produce a similar house; in the same manner, if the artificer would know in particular the very house which is to be made, so that nothing else would concur to make it similar to the house to be built, the artificer could, by thus knowing in particular the house to be made, produce it just as perfectly or more perfectly than if he knew another house. In this manner, the very house itself, as foreknown, is the exemplar of itself. And this is the case with God. God knows the very same things which He afterwards produces. And He looks to them in producing, and is precisely called a rational creator because He produces by looking at them and He knows perfectly, not in general only but in particular and most distinctly, whatever He produces.

With regard to the third part of the doubt, it is evident that by virtue of the connotation of the term[25] it can be conceded that the eternal existence of the idea is not any different from the existence of the stone which was produced in time; because an idea had an existence from eternity, in so far as it was known by God from eternity.

Nevertheless, while according to the usage of the saints it is conceded that the ideas are from eternity, that is, are known by God from eternity, it is not conceded by them that the stone that exists has existed from eternity. And, therefore, according to the usage of the saints, the stone was not existential from eternity in the same sense as has been the idea. In other words, the saints do not admit that the stone which exists was existential from eternity, although they do admit that the ideas existed from eternity.

As to Seneca, I say that his meaning is the same as that of Saint Augustine. He intends to say that God has within Himself numbers, etc., as objects known. And that is why he uses the expression "holding in His mind," because he desires to imply that He does not have them, except as known objects. And in that sense are they immortal, etc., as was explained before.

To the fourth part of the doubt, I say that by virtue of the connotation of the term it must be admitted that ideas arise and perish, because the ideas are the created things themselves which arise and perish. And nevertheless, according to the conception of Saint Augustine, they neither perish nor arise; that is, they neither begin to be understood by God originally, nor

[25] In the original: "de virtute sermonis," indicating that the word can carry that meaning. The expression coincides with the modern phrase: "in a literal sense" or "literally."

do they cease to be understood by God, but they are always and eternally understood. This view differentiates the ideas of God from the ideas in the mind of any created artificer in whose mind ideas originate and perish, that is, they cease to be understood by the artificer.

To the third doubt, I say that the ideas are precisely of singular objects, because precisely singular objects are producible. And if Plato says that the ideas are ideas of the species and not of singular objects, we have to interpret him in this manner, that perhaps in his opinion God does not know the singular objects, but only the species of singular objects. In that case Plato wished to say that the ideas are not ideas of singular objects; that is, they are not understood through the singular objects themselves, but that ideas are ideas of the species, that is, of the species of singular objects. But if Plato taught this, he erred, and Saint Augustine does not follow him in this point but in other things in which Plato did not err.

To the last doubt, I say that although God has a higher efficacy in acting than the created artificer, He is of an infinitely higher intelligence also. For that reason, God has not only a knowledge of the universals with reference to the things which He will produce, as the created artificer has about the things he intends to make; but God also has a distinct and particular knowledge of any particular thing to be produced, and, therefore, to Him the very particular thing is the idea. Yet God knows whatever is being known by a created agent. And for that reason, besides the ideas which are the particular things, we have to posit others, which are rightly the ideas of some things to be made, ideas, to be sure, not for God, but for created artificers.[26] For one and the same thing can be idea to somebody and yet not be an idea with regard to someone else, as the same thing may be an exemplar to one, and not an exemplar to another. And if it will be said that, according to the foregoing, God intuits something outside Himself to create according to it what He creates, a view contrary to Saint Augustine, my answer is this: God does not intuit anything which exists actually by itself in order to produce according to it. He has no foreknowledge of anything actually existing so that His intuition would be conditioned by it. Yet He intuits something which is not Himself, and is not something real, but can become real so that He would produce the thing according to the very thing itself.

If it is retorted that in that case God would be in need of something other than Himself in order to produce, which view is absurd, my reply would be the following: God is not in need of anything, because nothing is required for His action. And, therefore, God does not need ideas in order to act, nor properly speaking are the ideas themselves necessary in order to enable Him to act. Only the knowledge of the ideas themselves is required, and that knowledge is identical with God in every way. Precisely because God is God: God knows everything and He could not be called a rational agent unless He would have a knowledge of what He performs.

The principal proposition now is evident: The idea is not a ground of knowing, but is that which is known.

[26] The original text reads: "et ita praeter ideas quae sunt res particulares est ponere alia quae sunt r'ctū (illegible) fiendorum aliquorum idee, non quidem deo quamvis sint idee artificibus creatis." The sense is that God knows not only His own ideas, but the ideas which are in the minds of human beings also.

NATURAL PHILOSOPHY

Ockham's works on natural philosophy, as yet neglected by modern scholars, were directly influential in raising the problems of the illustrious physical school of Parisian nominalists represented by John Buridan (d. 1358), Albert of Saxony (d. 1390), and Marsilius of Inghen (d. 1396), who in their turn became the pioneers of modern mechanics founded by Galileo (d. 1642). Ockham's theory of motion was even more far reaching. With it he was among the first to anticipate the law of gravitation and inertia and Newton's (d. 1727) laws of motion. His doctrine of infinity found an echo in the works of Copernicus (d. 1543) and Bruno (d. 1600). His insistence upon the homogeneousness of the universe against the chorus of medieval cosmologists was to bear fruit later in Nicolaus of Cusa (d. 1464).

I T IS false to say that in unchanging things we can attain by one unique operation that magnitude which is the smallest or the greatest. Contrarily, and this is the true opinion, in every permanent thing which is infinitely divisible, such as are all continuous objects and all qualities subject to motion, there is according to many no minimum, because no matter how small the given particle may be, divine power could produce an even smaller one. In the same way, there is no maximum because no matter how great a previous datum, a still greater one might have been given.

To the rejoinder that in the case of any given thing it remains true that it could actually be produced by a single operation, I have no objection, just as little objection as to the view that in any division of a continuous object its datum could be actualized by a unique operation.

If it be retorted that the possibility of such a datum is not the possibility of something in becoming,[1] but of

[1] In the original: "in fieri."

something in completed fact,[2] I reply that if one takes the possibility of something in completed fact in the sense of a simple reduction of that possibility to actuality so that no further potentiality remains, such a notion of possibility in actuality should be rejected. We never really can attain to the infinite nor to anything which has realized in actuality all that was in potentiality; in truth, this potentiality is never exhausted without there remaining always a possibility for a new becoming.[3]

In this matter the authority of the Philosopher should not be accepted. He restricts the limits of such augmentation too narrowly. One of his contentions is that it would be a contradiction to assume the increase of water filling the sphere. Yet, God could make another world; in fact, it is my belief that God could not make so many worlds as not to be able to make additional ones. It would not be a contradiction to suppose that God could out of all these waters make one water.[4] I do not see why God could not add to any finite amount of actual water another drop of water.[5]

Such an infinite process is not to be denied unless it be followed by some infinity of creation. Over and beyond any given fire God can make a greater fire, and yet he cannot make infinite fire. It is impossible that God should make so many individuals of the same order that he could not make any more, and yet he cannot make an infinite number of individuals outright.[6] Given any individual thing God can make an-

[2] In the original: "in facto esse."
[3] *Sent.* I, dist. 17, qu. 8, T.
[4] *Sent.* I, dist. 17, qu. 8, Y.
[5] *Sent.* I, dist. 17, qu. 8, H.
[6] *Sent.* I, dist. 17, qu. 8, C .

other individual of the same order without previously destroying the existing ones.[7]   Therefore, it is not necessary to deny an infinite process in order to avoid infinity.   The reason is that if we suppose such a process to infinity, that which is actualized will always be finite and, therefore, God, by making always more, would never make infinite things but finite ones.[8]

⌐ To this point I add that there is no such a thing as a natural minimum which could not (at least by divine power) be further divided into smaller parts to infinity, retaining throughout its natural sameness.[9]

Concerning the proposition that the first cause cannot make many worlds, I hold as the most probable opinion the one which says that God is able to make another world better than ours and distinct in kind from it.[10]   The reason for this is that God can produce an infinite number of individual beings of the same order as, and in addition to, those already in existence. Since, however, his creativeness is not limited to this world, he can produce them outside of this world—making thus of them another world, just as he made this world out of things already produced.[11]

It may be objected, as the Philosopher does in his work on *Heaven and the World,* that if there were another world, then the earth of that world would either move toward the center of this world or not.   It cannot be said that it would not, because bodies of the same element move to the same place; therefore, because the earth of this world moves by nature toward the center of this world, the earth of that other world would move by nature toward the center of this world also.

[7] *Sent.* I, dist. 17, qu. 8, G.   [8] *Sent.* I, dist. 17, qu. 8, D.
[9] *Sent.* II, qu. 8, G.   [10] *Sent.* I, dist. 44, D.
[11] *Sent.* I, dist. 44, E.

If, however, the earth of the other world does not
move toward the center of this world, then, by its nature, it recedes from the center of this world. But this
is impossible, because no heavy body ever moves by
nature from the center.

If to this point it is replied that the individual objects of the same element move by nature to the center
yet not identically to the same but each to its own
center even though these be numerically diverse, the
Philosopher answers that this would be impossible,
because, then, the different parts of our earth would
move toward various centers, the opposite of which is
apparent to our senses.

To this I answer: All individual objects of the same
element could by their nature move toward exactly the
same place, in case they occupied successively the same
spot lying outside their natural place. Nevertheless,
there is no reason why they should always move toward
the same place. It is possible that they move simultaneously toward diverse places. This can be seen in
the instance of two fires consisting of the same elements, placed in various parts of the earth which move
toward the circumference of the heaven. They do not
move toward the same place but to different ones. If,
however, one of them were transferred to the place
where the other was, then, of course, both would move
identically toward the same place. Exactly this would
happen if the earth of the other world were put where
the earth is within this heaven. It would move toward
the same place as does the earth of this world. Considering, however, that it is outside of this world and
within the heaven of another world, it will just as
little move toward the center of this world, as a fire

going up at Oxford would move identically toward the same place as if it were at Paris.[12]

Motion may be taken in a wider and in a stricter sense. In the wide sense it is understood as a sudden mutation; in the stricter sense, it is taken for whatever is distinguished from a sudden mutation.[13] To change means to be in a state different from the previous one. For this it is sufficient to have permanent things so that one is in the place of the other when the former is not there, or that one is not present where it was before. In order to have the air obscured it is sufficient that the light cease in the air by the removal of its cause without inserting any thing to be destroyed suddenly. This makes it plain that when a thing changes into a form which it did not have before, it is not necessary to suppose two forms: a permanent and a transient one. A single form which was not there before, is adequate to explain the notion of change. There is no need to posit transient things besides the permanent things which endure through time; and, therefore, change is not the destruction of a thing so transient as to endure for but an instant.[14]

Motion is defined as the act of an existent in potentiality in so far as it is in potentiality. This means that when some moving body has actively achieved one place it has a potentiality to be in another place toward which it is heading.[15] Motion is not a thing totally distinguished by itself from permanent things. It is not an absolute thing; for if it were, it would be either a substance or quantity. Obviously, it is not substance. Nor could it be a quantity; because then when a thing moved, it would swell or diminish its quantity which

[12] *Sent.* I, dist. 44, F.   [14] *Summulae in Phys.* III, 3.
[13] *Summulae in Phys.* III, 2.   [15] *Summulae in Phys.* III, 5.

is absurd. Much less could it be a quality or a relation. Consequently, motion cannot itself be a thing.[16]

Having shown that motion is not an entity apart
from the things which remain permanent, let us inquire what motion is.

For the concept of motion it is sufficient that the
body in question move continuously, without being in-
terrupted by time or rest, one state succeeding another
in a divisible manner. Just as for the concept of
"whitening," it is enough that the thing should continuously assemble the parts of whiteness, for local motion it is enough that the mobile body be continuously
without rest in diverse places successively. This brings
out clearly that for motion nothing is required besides
permanent things, and makes evident, consequently,
that motion is not an entity apart from permanent
things.[17] If we sought precision by using words like
"mover," "moved," "movable," and the like instead of
words like "motion," "mobility," and others of the
kind, many difficulties and doubts would be excluded.

Motion does not differ from the thing moved, as
Aristotle puts it in calling motion a certain kind of
flux. This saying can be understood in a twofold manner. In one sense, it means that motion is a thing
distinct from all permanent things, flowing continuously from non-being to being; in the other sense, it
means that one part of being continuously passes, another continuously succeeds in the nature of things.
This is the far-famed way of conceiving motion which
I think represents the notion of the Philosopher and
the Commentator (i. e., Averroes).[18]

Yet bodies moving in space do not acquire anything

16 *Summulae in Phys.,* III, 5. 17 *Summulae in Phys.,* III, 6.
18 *Summulae in Phys.,* III, 7.

inherent. If you insist that the moving body does not move unless it acquires something which it did not have before, I answer that it has something new, not as inherent to it as to a substance, but it has acquired a different location. And if you further inquire as to what is necessary for the body to be in that place, I reply that nothing else is required but a body and a place and the absence of any intermediary moving sometimes in one direction, sometimes in the opposite direction.[19]

We have to bring to our attention the great difficulty involved in the explanation of projectile motion, with reference to its impelling and efficient principle. This cannot be the projector, who could disappear while the motion continues; nor the air which could move contrarily, as when the arrow hits a stone; nor any force in, say, the projected stone. What, indeed, could cause this force? Not the projector, because he as active agent approaches equally, whether slowly or rapidly, the object to be thrown. Therefore, I say that in such a motion, after the separation from the original projector has occurred, the moving body itself is the motion on its own account and not by some absolute force bearing upon it. To sum up: the thing moving and the movement are thoroughly indistinguishable.[20]

It is not universally true that the mover and the moved must be simultaneously together by mathematical contact.[21] It will prove that they can be distant from each other.

An illustration is furnished by the magnet. In my opinion the magnet attracts the iron which is spatially

[19] *Summulae in Phys.*, III, 7.
[20] *Sent.* II, qu. 26, M.
[21] *Sent.* II, qu. 18, J.

distant from it not by virtue of something existing in the intermediary space or in the iron, but directly. This magnetic stone, then, acts directly through the distance without utilizing a medium.

The conclusion is evident. Let us suppose that some force produced in the iron by the magnet should actually move the iron. In that event, I should say that if the causing agent and the caused result are the same, other things remaining unchanged, the same effect should always follow. If, now, it is the force in the iron and not the magnet which moves the iron, the iron should continue to move itself by virtue of the potentiality engendered in it, even after the magnet were destroyed by divine power. But, then, I ask: in what direction? It might move upwards or in a horizontal line or in some other way. Neither of these could happen, and I can prove it. The force, indeed, does not move upward unless the magnetic stone is above, and the same thing is true as regards other spatial directions. But if the magnetic stone were destroyed by the power of God, there would be no motion upwards or otherwise, even though the iron had conserved its force. And so it is not a force existing in the iron which is the moving principle but the magnetic stone itself. In the same way it is proved that no force of the magnetic stone preserved in intermediary space by God after the destruction of the magnet could move the iron. Such force could not move the iron in any direction, because the iron cannot move except in the direction of the magnet.[22] Therefore, the magnet is the immediate cause of this motion and the total cause in so far as a secondary cause, that is a created thing, can be a total cause.[23]

[22] *Sent*. II, qu. 18, E.   [23] *Sent*. II, qu. 26, H.

ETHICAL PHILOSOPHY

A study of Ockham's Ethics reveals to us the deep undertow which carries the whole current of his philosophy. Its dominant tone is given in an insistent voluntarism in which the inner experiences of his impetuous nature found expression. For Ockham the foundations of morality were given in the will of God, unrestricted by any normative divine essence conceived of in intellectualistic terms. This view, extended to cosmic dimensions, leaves way to chance and to the unpredictable elements of an emerging process.

O UR understanding of the intellectual soul as an immaterial and incorruptible form which is totally in the whole and totally in every part, cannot be accepted as evident from either reason or experience. We cannot know whether such a form is in us, or that it is the nature of such substance in us to be intellectual, or that the soul is the form of the body. I do not care how Aristotle felt about this, because everywhere he himself appears on this point to be uncertain. We hold the three foregoing propositions only by faith.[1]

The potentialities of the soul, that is, the intellect and the will, leaving the sensitive potentialities unmentioned, are really identical in relation to each other and with the essence of the soul. The intellect is no more distinguished from the will than from itself, no more than God from God, no more than a strong man from a strong man. It is not distinguished from the will either in reality or by reason. But now the manner in which the substance of the soul can have acts distinguished by reason with their respective words having different connotations is this, in so far as it elicits or may elicit acts of understanding, it is called intellect,

[1] *Quodlib.* I, qu. 10.

and in so far as it elicits acts of volition, it is called will.[2]

If we take will for the actual thing which is designated by the word or concept as meaning the principle which elicits the acts of volition and cognition, the will is not more superior to the intellect than the intellect is superior to the will, both being altogether the same. Taking both, however, with reference to what their names signify, the will may be called superior to the intellect, because the act of loving, designated by the word will, is superior to the act of understanding, designated by the word intellect.[3]

There is no necessarily conclusive reason why the intellect should be declared active, when it is only passive.[4] In case of necessary propositions, known by themselves, the assent is caused sufficiently by the knowledge of the simple terms and the apprehension of the complex terms without any act by the intellect of its own.[5] The immediate cause of both the sensitive and the intellectual cognition may be the volition. Whether, now, the potentialities of cognitive acts are active or passive, the grade of intensity, of the conatus or attention in our cognition, cannot be caused at all without the act of the will. There is no necessity of adopting the view of active cognitive potentialities because no plurality is to be accepted without necessity. Taking the intellect as purely passive, everything can be explained by the act of will or by the object or by the impression of things.[6] Therefore, I say that the cause, as a result of which a true rather than a false

[2] *Sent.* II, qu. 24, K.
[3] *Sent.* II, qu. 24, P.
[4] *Sent.* II, qu. 25, A.
[5] *Sent.* II, qu. 25, L.
[6] *Sent.* II, qu. 26, U.

proposition is formed, an affirmative rather than a negative, is the will, because the will wants to form the one and not the other.[7]

The will with respect to a simple object or a complex object, such as "to be happy" or "to want to be," is called love. Not to will the same, may be called hatred or detestation.[8] As the ultimate end, we may accept either the possible created happiness of the will or the object of this happiness. With reference to this happiness, be it shown in general or in particular, along the earthly trail or in the heavenly home; I say that the will, absolutely speaking, may want it or not want it.[9]

The will is not necessarily attracted by the ultimate end shown in general. Natural necessity does not stand together with freedom.[10] Freedom is opposed to necessity in the same way as necessity is opposed to contingency. Thus, freedom is some kind of indifference and contingency[10a] and is distinguished against the natural active principle."[11] Nature and will are two active principles with opposed modes of origination. Because the mode as nature originates cannot stand with the mode as the will originates,[11a] which intends the end freely, it follows that it cannot intend the end with natural necessity. The assumption that the will intends the end freely can be proven thus. It is one and

[7] *Sent.* II, qu. 25, K.

[8] *Sent.* I, dist. 1, qu. 6, O.

[9] *Sent.* I, dist. 2, qu. 1, U.

[10] *Sent.* I, dist. 1, qu. 6, B.

[10a] In the original: "libertas est quaedam indifferentia et contingentia."

[11] *Sent.* I, dist. 2, qu. 1, U.

[11a] In the original: "natura et voluntas sunt principia activa habentia oppositum modum principiandi; ergo cum modo principiandi voluntatis non stat modus principiandi naturae . . ."

the same potentiality which intends the end and that
which is in behalf of this end. Therefore, it has the
same mode of acting because different modes would
indicate different potentialities. But we see it operat-
ing freely in matters which promote the end. Consequently, it acts in the same manner to attain the end.[12]
It is to be denied, then, that everything by nature's
necessity has an inclination, in strict sense of the word,
toward its own perfection. This is true only if the
thing to be perfected is active by natural necessity,
which cannot be said about the will.[13]

The will is attracted by the ultimate end shown in
general in a contingent and free manner, as we explained it. This is to say that the will may like happiness and may not like it; may desire happiness and may
not. This is evident from the fact that many believers, with faith in the future life, just as well as unbelievers, without faith in any future life, have killed
themselves with the full use of their reason; have
thrown themselves into the arms of death; these alike
have not wanted to exist. And it is true, in the same
way, that some may not desire happiness in specific
instances. Whoever wants something efficaciously,
wants everything also without which in his opinion the
desired object cannot be obtained at all. Yet some of
the faithful are convinced that they cannot attain happiness without a good life, and still they do not culti-
vate a good and saintly life. Therefore, they do not
desire happiness efficiently and, consequently, with the
same reason, they may not want it.[14]

It may be said, then, that the will is free with regard

[12] *Sent.* I, dist. 2, qu. 1, B.
[13] *Sent.* I, dist. 2, qu. 1, X.
[14] *Sent.* I, dist. 2, qu. 1, P-T.

to any act elicited by the same, if we consider the matter absolutely. It is to be noted, however, that by considering some act, inasmuch as it is caused by a habit, and is antecedent in the will, the will is not free with reference to that act.[15]

It cannot be proved that some effect is actually produced by a second cause. Although burning always follows the contact of fire with an inflammable object, this does not exclude the possibility that its cause is not the fire. It may be that God has so ordained things that whenever fire is compresent to the object, He himself is the cause of burning. There is no effect which could prove that somebody is a human being, especially if we consider effects as they appear to us. Whatever we see that a man does, like eating, drinking and so on, an angel may do in a body also, as the instance of the angel of Tobiah teaches. It is little wonder, therefore, that we cannot demonstrate whether something is a cause or not.[16]

It is the will of God just as much as the essence of God that is the immediate cause of everything that happens, although with natural reason we cannot demonstrate this. This view may be recommended, however, in the following manner.[17]

God is the first and immediate cause of everything that is produced by secondary causes. An immediate cause is, obviously, one by the presence of which the effect can follow and by the absence of which the effect cannot follow. Now God is such a cause with respect to any created thing.[18] Properly speaking any cause,

[15] *Sent*. III, qu. 4, N.
[16] *Sent*. II, qu. 5, R. S.
[17] *Sent*. I, dist. 25, qu. unica G.
[18] *Sent*. II, qu. 5, K.

in the proper sense of the word, that is, a phenomenon
in the presence of which the effect follows and in the
absence of which the effect does not follow, may be
called immediate cause. When, therefore, God con-
curs with a second cause, both are immediate causes.
God is the immediate cause of any effect because He is
the first cause by virtue of the priority of perfection
but not by virtue of the priority of duration. For in
the same moment that He acts the second cause acts
also with the consequence that He is partial cause of
any effect produced by the secondary cause.[19] God by
concurring in the second cause, although He would be
able to produce the effect without the second cause and,
consequently, would be the total cause, does, however,
as a matter of fact, produce it with the second cause.
Consequently, God is not, in fact, the total cause. It is
manifest, then, that God is immediately the first and
direct cause of any effect produced by secondary
causes.[20]

Although God acts through the mediacy of secondary
causes, or, more strictly, with them, we should not say
that He acts mediately or that secondary causes are superfluous. In the case of man, he is a voluntary, not a
necessitated agent; and even if he were necessitated,
God would still act immediately. God acts in such a
way that though He could be the total cause of the effect without anything else, nevertheless, in His administration, things have their own movements, as Saint
Augustine teaches. God does not want to produce the
whole effect alone but as a partial cause to be a co-
agent with the secondary causes, although He is superior. Therefore, He is the immediate cause of every-

[19] *Sent.* II, qu. 5, L.
[20] *Sent.* II, qu. 5, M.

thing both when He acts with other causes and when He acts without them.   The secondary causes, meanwhile, cannot be called superfluous, because God reveals His power through them in a different manner.[21]

If it could be proven that God intends something which is not Himself, it might be proven that the divine will is always realized.   However, it cannot be proven that whatever is intended by God is done by God, nor that whatever is intended by God is done by somebody else.[22]   It cannot be proven by natural reason that God is the immediate cause of everything, nor that he is not the immediate cause of everything.   There is no proof whatever in the light of natural reason that God is the total cause of anything.   There is no proof, therefore, from natural reason that whatever God intends is done by God, nor that whatever is intended by God is done by somebody else.   Since, then, it cannot be demonstrated by natural reason that God is the immediate cause of everything, it cannot be established whether or not the divine will is always realized by Himself or by somebody else.[23]

In the same manner, it is a matter of belief that God is a free cause with regard to everything.   It cannot be so demonstrated by natural reason that the unbelievers may not gainsay it.   Nevertheless, it may be recommended in this way.   Every cause which cannot be impeded may face everything, in fact, infinity itself in an equal manner.   If at a given moment it actualizes one of the many possibilities, no other reason than its being a free agent can be given for its producing one effect rather than another.   But God is such a cause

[21] *Sent.* II, qu. 5, R.
[22] *Sent.* I, dis. 46, qu. 2, C.
[23] *Sent.* I, dist. 46, qu. 2, E, F.

180   OCKHAM

with respect to all things produced by Him from eternity.[24] Therefore, it is to be accepted as a fact that God is a cause which acts contingently. He may do otherwise than He does because any agent acting contingently may act otherwise. In the same way, God can produce souls in infinite number, because He does not have to stop at a given number. Nevertheless, He does not produce souls in an infinite, but only in a given, quantity.[25]

God cannot be obligated to any act. It would not constitute sin even though God were to commit as a total cause the acts which He now performs with the sinner as a partial cause. "Sin is nothing else than an act of commission or omission when there is an obligation for man. Only obligation constitutes one a sinner or not a sinner." But God cannot be obligated to any act. With Him a thing becomes right solely for the reason that He wants it to be so. If God as a total cause were to instigate hatred toward Himself in the will of somebody—just as He now causes it as a partial cause—such a person would not be guilty of sin and neither would God, because He is not obligated to anything. In this case the person would not be obligated either, because his act would not be in his control.[26]

Hatred of God, stealing, adultery, and the like, of course, have sinful circumstances connected with them according to the generally accepted law, inasmuch as the person who performs them is obligated by divine precept to the contrary. As far as the absolute being of those acts is concerned, however, they may be performed by God without any sinful circumstance at-

[24] *Sent.* II, dist. 43, qu. 1, M, N.
[25] *Sent.* I, dist. 43, qu. 1, M. N.
[26] *Sent.* II, qu. 9, F.

tached to them.   They may even be meritoriously performed by man if they fall under divine precept, just
as now their opposites, as a matter of fact, fall under
the divine precept.[27]

Moral goodness and malice involve the obligation of
an agent to a certain act or to its opposite.[28] Sin does
not exist except in an act of will.   In the same way,
merit cannot be assumed except for the will at least in
part.[29]

Nothing occurring in a man living in mortal sin is
the effect of predestination.   To the contrary, good
deeds performed in the state of mortal sin are in some
way the cause why God grants His grace.[30] The ground,
moreover, why God predestines some for that reason and others without any reason is merely God's will
to do so.   The reason why Saint Paul was struck by
God and converted without any previous merits of his
own while others were not, is nothing else than the will
of God.[31]

[27] *Sent.* II, qu. 19, N. O.
[28] *Sent.* II, qu. 19, P.
[29] *Sent.* III, qu. 4, M.
[30] *Sent.* I, dist. 41, qu. 1, G.
[31] Ibid.

PHILOSOPHY OF RELIGION

Ockham's philosophy of religion reveals his basically critical and sceptical attitude in its most searching form. At the same time it discloses his utter intellectual honesty and fearlessness. Rational theology and psychology received mortal wounds from the nominalistic approach. As a result, faith found a refuge in the mysticism of the late scholastic period or, later, forgot itself in the ethical individualism of the Renaissance.

The following gives Ockham's analysis of the conception of God taken from the second question of the third distinction in his Commentary to the first book of the *Sentences*. It contains the whole passage from marginal letter E to M uninterruptedly. Another important illustration of his philosophy of religion will be given in the first three of his "Hundred Theological Sayings" or "Centilogium Theologicum."

SOMETHING is known in itself when nothing else but that thing alone terminates the act of intellect, not any other thing, distinguished from it by reason or by real differentiation. Such a thing may be known abstractly or intuitively. Another way of knowing a thing is to know it, not in itself, but in a certain concept of its own. This is most truly so when this concept is found verified with regard to that thing. And it is in this way that we have to understand the statement of the Philosopher in the second book of the *Posterior Analytics* where he says that sometimes when we know a thing we can know, that it *is* and *what* it is at the same time. His reason is that such a thing, because we do not know its essence, or at least part of its essence, yields a superficial knowledge. But about that we shall discourse at another place.

Now when something is known in a certain concept of its own we know first that it *is* before we know *what* it is, that is, before we know its essence with a proper or equivalent cognition or any part of its essence or any simple element of it. If fire would be known in itself, seeing the fire, we would know that it is fire and what fire is. As a matter of fact, however, fire is not known in itself but only the accident of fire. The case is different with heat which is known that it is and what it is, and such is the case with all the accidents which terminate the act of intellect directly. In other instances where we do not know in this manner, we know first that the thing *is* before we know *what* it is. Thus, we know first that something is located between the sun and the moon before we know what it is which is located between.

After these preliminaries I am setting up the following propositions with reference to the question:

First, that neither the divine essence, nor the divine quiddity, nor anything intrinsic to God, nor anything that is really God, can be known without involving something else along with the knowledge of God.

Second, the divine essence or the divine quiddity can be known by us in a concept of its own, which, to be sure, is a composite concept, the parts of which are able to be abstracted naturally from the things.

Third, the divine essence can be known by us in a uniquely simple concept which is instituted arbitrarily for signification and is connotative and negative in an exclusive manner.

The first proposition is evident, for nothing can be known in itself through natural channels unless it is known intuitively; but God cannot be known by us intuitively through purely natural channels and so to the conclusion. The minor is manifest. The major is

proved in this manner: there is no stronger reason
why one thing should be known by us in itself without
previous intuitive knowledge rather than another thing;
but many things are knowable only with a previous intuitive knowledge, because according to the Philosopher, a man born blind cannot have a knowledge of
colors, nor can he know color in itself because he cannot know color intuitively. Therefore, generally, no
thing can be known unless it is preliminarily known by
intuition. Now, if a created thing cannot be known in
itself save as it is first known intuitively, how much
more must this be true of God!

The second proposition is evident. Just as any created thing may be known by some simple general concept, so can God, for otherwise He could not be known
by us at all. Now, there are many general traits each
having a certain content which taken together result in
a single concept appropriate to Him. And because
these general traits are distinctly separate, it is necessary that some content would be proper to every single
one which does not correspond to any of the rest. These
several distinct general traits as coalesced in one cannot be attributed to anything else. Now there are many
simple notions common to God and something else
which can be abstracted naturally, every one of which
is common to God and to something else. All these
taken together make one concept appropriate to God.
Moreover, as this concept can be understood as verifi-
able of somebody, it is God that is known in that concept.

To clarify by example: We can abstract from entities
the concept of being because it is common to God and
all other entities. In the same way, we can abstract

the concept of wisdom because it is precisely common to created and uncreated wisdom. Similarly can we abstract the concept of goodness which is precisely common to divine and created goodness. Note that in all this, goodness is distinguished from wisdom. Now all these concepts together cannot be verified except in God alone, because, by definition, the created wisdom is not the created goodness, nor conversely, although we may say that some entity is goodness or is wisdom and so with the rest which are called attributes. This brings out clearly how God is known in a concept of His own. What we mean to say is that many concepts can be abstracted from the created things which are common to God and the creatures from which we may conclude to one composite concept proper to God. We abstracted the notion of being, the notion of goodness, wisdom, love, and the rest, and we concluded from any particular entities to goodness, wisdom, love, justice, and so on, and then we recognized God in a general concept of His own. Nevertheless, God himself is not directly known, because something else than God is known. All the terms of the propositions, "There is an entity which is wisdom, justice, love, and so on," are concepts none of which is really God. We know all these terms and the proposition made out of them, yet through them we know something else than God. And the case is the same with reference to all other propositions, too, which are possible to us.

To the third proposition I say that God can be known by us in a simple, connotative, and negative concept of His own. This knowledge is not different from the one when we know a simple concept derived from any individual entity. We can know that there is a being which is first simply so, that there is a being which is creative or first cause or pure actuality, or that there is a being which is immortal, incorruptible, unconditioned, uncaused, and so about the rest. This concept is a simple one although it signifies distinct features primarily or secondarily, in other words, directly or indirectly.

But against the afore-mentioned propositions there are certain doubts. The first is that to know a thing in something else does not seem to be possible. By the denotation of something which is altogether extrinsic to another thing we do not denote the latter. Therefore, from the fact that we know the concept does not follow that the real thing is known.

To this my answer is as follows: it may be said that we know something by extrinsic denotation by realizing that a thing which we know immediately is related to something not immediately known as its property, so that the former stands and suppots for the latter. It would be wrong to conclude that there is no God. Nor does it follow that by knowing the concept we do not know God either mediately or immediately. But it follows that owing to this situation God is not known directly and in Himself but is well known in something else. Because I cannot know God in Himself we employ for Him a concept of His own and attribute to this concept whatever can be attributed to God. By doing this, however, we do not stop at the concept but refer the concept to God. We predicate this concept not of itself but of God with regard to all the things which could be predicated of God if He would be known in Himself. Whether this predication is a proper or improper one I do not care right now.

To this point I say that we cannot know in itself

either the oneness of God, or His firstness, or His infinite power, or divine goodness and perfection. The things which we know about Him immediately, are certain concepts, which in reality are not God, which, however, we use in propositions for God. Through them we know by a general cognition many other things besides God; and, therefore, that entity which is God, or that simple power or perfection which is God, cannot be known by us in itself.

FROM THE HUNDRED THEOLOGICAL
SAYINGS

The *Centilogium Theologicum* of Ockham was first printed
in 1495 in Lyons, France, by John Trechsel the German. It is
attached to the voluminous Commentary to the *Sentences,* one
of Ockham's earliest works also printed in 1495 in Lyons. The
sceptical tone of Ockham's *Theological Sayings* is typical of
the late Scholastic period. His criticism of the cosmological
argument for the existence of God is an early anticipation of
Kant's Fourth Antinomy.

THE SOUL inborn in us is imbued with a natural
longing to know its goal over and above the rest
of corruptible, created, appetitive beings, because of
its endowment with reason and of its higher and more
excellent image and similitude of God. This fact will
be especially confirmed by a consideration of what
Aristotle says in the first book of the *Ethics* where we
learn that all the arts and all doctrine, and, in the same
manner, all acts and the intellect, too, seem to be striv-
ing after some good. This good is manifested to us
by divine wisdom whose beautiful instructions reveal
to us the ultimate end of man which is God. He is the
Alpha and Omega, the beginning and end, and to His
praise and glory I will propound very shortly and aptly
a hundred theological sayings, the first of which is as
follows:

There is a God. This conclusion is held unanimously
by theologians and philosophers. In theology it is
established as a first principle, presupposed by all and
accepted as the foundation of all other conclusions.
In philosophy the same proposition is not only held by
many as an opinion but is demonstrated also by appeal
to the physical world, as is done in the seventh book

of Aristotle's *Physics*. Here he argues from natural
principles to an altogether immobile first mover which
is called by everyone first cause and God. He says the
same thing in the second book of his *Metaphysics*,
where Aristotle declares that in causes there is no regress to infinity, and, consequently, we have to arrive
at a first cause which is the supreme good for all. He
deduces the same conclusion with even greater clarity
in the twelfth book of the *Metaphysics* where he proves
that all things have one principle, i. e., a first and most
perfect substance which is called God by all. Hence,
at the outset, as the basis of this whole work, I posit
this conclusion, presupposed and stated by both philosophers and theologians.

When it comes to ascertaining, however, the necessity of positing this, in other words, whether it is de-
monstrable or probable that there is a God, and,
whether this is a self-evident proposition or not, the
conclusion is not equally as evident. And, therefore,
I judge it to be worth while to discuss this matter.
However, I want to make a preliminary declaration
that if I should state something in this booklet or in
some other book of mine which is not fitting, I will
make a recantation with regard to such writings now
as well as then.

Now Aristotle deduces the first mobile mover in the
eighth book of the *Physics* in this manner: Whatever
moves is moved by some other agent; but there is no
regress in causes to infinity; therefore, there is in moving things a first mover itself unmoved. The first part
of the antecedent, to wit, that whatever is moved is
moved by some other agent, is evident from the fact
that otherwise it would follow that something could
move itself, originally and by itself, and thus, that thing

would be actual and potential from the same point of view. The second part of the antecedent, to wit, that there is no infinite regression in causes of motion is evident from the fact that if there were an infinite procession there would be no intermediary cause, because where there is no ultimate, there is no intermediate cause either. And this seems to be an *a posteriori* demonstration because it begins from the effect, that is, from the motion.

But this argument, although for some it may appear probable, does not seem to be conclusive. First, because I can reasonably say that something moves itself, for instance, the soul and the angels, who produce their various actions, and weight (*gravitas*) itself which descends by moving itself. And if it is said that this descension is conditioned by the descending subject and thus the weight does not move itself, my reply is this: we rather call something moving which moves by moving itself than the thing to which movement adheres, that is, its subject. Therefore, the cause of motion is precisely the natural act of descending which keeps on descending even while its subject is being described. The same thing is apparent in the sacrament of the Altar where, according to many, the accidents are posited without a subject.[1]

To some, then, it does not seem to be inappropriate that something could move itself and, consequently, this proposition, "whatever moves is moved by some other agent," is not self-evident, nor is it deduced from self-evident propositions, and consequently it is not a demonstrative principle.

[1] That is, just as in the Eucharist the invisible substance of the bread and wine is separable from the phenomena of the accidents, in the same manner, movement and the moving body can be considered as separable.

To the opposite argument, that from this it would follow that one and the same thing would be actuality and potentiality at once, such is the answer: This proposition may have a twofold sense: one, that the same thing has some character actually and does not have it actually, but has it potentially. This sense is impossible as involving manifest contradiction. The other sense, according to which a thing may have some character actually and potentially tends to cause in itself something which it is capable of becoming, seems to many to be quite possible. And this is sufficient to cancel the fact that the afore-mentioned proposition, "whatever moves is moved by some other agent," is a first principle. Other reasons of Aristotle whereby he tries to prove the same thing, although they seem to be probable to many, yet are not considered by everybody as demonstrative.

In the second place, one can assail the other assumed proposition which states that "there is no infinite regress in the series of movers." Undoubtedly in certain series of causes infinite regress must be admitted. For instance, if some linear continuum is struck by percussion at a point, then that terminal point which is struck moves the adjacent part, and that part another one, and so on to infinity. In that way there will be an infinite number of parts, at least proportionately so, according to the length, every one of them being moved by reason of such percussion. Thus, we can see that it is not impossible but rather necessary to admit in moving things an infinite regress. In discontinuous things, on the other hand, in which no linear continuity is possible, infinity is not only tenable, but even more in accord with the principles of Aristotle. A case would be that of the intellectual souls, which are as-

sumed by Aristotle, in the second book of his treatise
On the Soul, to be perpetual and thus most probably
infinite.   In this manner men originated in infinite
numbers, a supposition well enough grounded unless
we are to assume one and the same soul in the multitude of man.

As to the second argument to the contrary, which
says that in case of an infinite process there would be
no intermediary cause with respect to the ultimate intrinsic principle, although some cause could be intermediary with respect to things not ultimate; or again
as to Aristotle's argument in the seventh book of the
Physics, where he comes to the conclusion that in case
of an infinite regress in causes of motion we would
have infinite motion in finite time, this is the answer:
To some it does not seem to be inappropriate to assume
such movement of infinite movers to be an infinite motion, because the moving elements may be incorporeal,
and even though they were corporeal the view that
their motion is infinite could yet be maintained.

From all this it follows, or seems to follow, that
Aristotle does not demonstrate the existence of an unmoved mover, although this view may be taken as more
probable than its opposite.   And the reason is that all
surface appearances can be saved equally well or even
better by positing a finite series in moving things and
one principle, rather than an infinite series; and for
that reason this view is to be preferred.

The second conclusion is that there is not a plurality
of gods, meaning by God the supreme good.   This conclusion is both theological and physical.   For in theology it is manifest that there is one God according to
the ten commandements given to Moses on Mount
Sinai and these commandments are binding for all

mortals generally, both by the old and the new law, as is proved from the book of *Exodus,* and briefly, throughout the whole of theology. The Philosopher, too, holds the same, as is shown plainly in the seventh book of the *Physics* where he arrives at one principle as evidenced in our first conclusion; in the first book *On the Heavens,* where he proves that there is not a plurality of worlds; and in the second book of the *Metaphysics* where he determines that there is one supreme and sempiternal cause.

This conclusion is accepted by all as probable and more probable than its opposite, yet it is not demonstrated at all. Theologically speaking, although we do not speak about an essential plurality in God, yet we posit a personal plurality and certainly some heretically posited essential plurality, as does Abbot Joachim* in his *Sum on the Trinity.*

Again from the point of view of reason, no inconvenience would result from the plurality of many causes. Among such causes there could not be any discordance, because every one of them would always work toward the best; and, consequently, they would govern everything by a unanimous consensus. Again, some people are quite dubious as to whether there is another world besides this one or not. For God could have created another or many other worlds just as easily as this, because by the creation of this world his potentiality was not altogether exhausted, as all theologians hold firmly. But then the question arises, if there is another world, why is there not another ruler, or first cause also?

*Joachim of Floris (1145-1202) an apocalyptic mystic abbot in Calabria. The allusion is made to his work *De unitate trinitatis.* This tritheistic treatise was condemned at the fourth Lateran Council held in 1215.

Neither are the arguments of Aristotle, propounded in the treatise *On the Heavens,* cogent to some. For his statement that the elements of this world would tend to move to the places of the elements of that other world, does not seem to be true. The contents of that world would have no influence upon this one because there would be no up or down or medium or ultimate or circumference or center with regard to this world— imagining, I mean, an earth purely extraneous to this world. Or if that world would be conceived having the same gravitational force as ours this would not necessitate any local difference in the movement there for it would be entirely a part of that world. The conclusion, then, is not demonstrated, but it may well be held as more probable than its opposite because all surface appearances appear equally[2] and can be saved easily by maintaining the unity of first cause. Therefore, we ought not assume such plurality.

The third conclusion is that God is infinitely intensive power.[3] This conclusion is to be believed and maintained firmly by theologians on the basis of what the word itself signifies as interpreted by Boethius in the fourth book of his *On the Consolation of Philosophy.* According to him, that than which nothing higher can be thought is of infinite power. Given, namely, anything finite, a still higher something can be conceived. The Philosopher, too, concludes the same thing in the eighth book of the *Physics* from the eternity of the first motion, where Aristotle seems to imply the impossibility of moving the first mobile thing perpetually, unless the first mover is of infinite power.

[2] In the original: "eo quod omnes apparentie equaliter apparent."

[3] In the original: "deus est intensive virtutis infinite."

The same view can be evinced from the second book of *Metaphysics* of Aristotle.

However, this conclusion seems by some not as demonstrated, but as a probable opinion only. First, what meaning the word here used has is entirely at the pleasure of those who employ it, because every name is a significatory word instituted at pleasure and, by consequence, does not introduce a necessity to admit this conclusion. Secondly, the argument of Aristotle does not prove nor does it introduce any evidence. The first mobile thing could be moved perpetually by an angel or by a soul or by any active potentiality no matter how small. For in that motion there is no resistance, either intrinsic or extrinsic; no intrinsic motion, because the first mobile thing is not a composition; no extrinsic motion, because here there is no medium which would create an obstacle and without a medium there cannot be any resistance, although certain definite things are required for motion. Again, Aristotle in the third book of the *Metaphysics* admits other movers of the spheres, too, capable of moving with their power although they are not of intensively infinite potentiality. The conclusion, therefore, is not demonstrated but is held only as a probable opinion. For it gives a sufficient honor to our God, if we acknowledge and attribute to him such excellency and glory as that than which nothing higher can be conceived.

POLITICAL PHILOSOPHY

Ockham's political philosophy with characteristic emphasis on the particular as against the universal presents a new evaluation of the human personality as against the corporate political body and an emphatic connecting of human rights with the laws of nature. With Marsilius of Padua (c. 1270-c. 1343) and John of Jandun (d. 1328), he was among the first to proclaim the sovereignty of the people as the source of all political power and to suggest the doctrine of the origin of the state through contract made by free individuals.

IN MATTERS of faith and of science I am more impressed by one evident reason or by one authoritative passage of the Holy Writ correctly understood than by the common chorus of mankind. I am not ashamed to be convinced by truth. In fact, to have truth victorious over me I estimate the most useful thing for me, but I never want to be defeated by the multitude. For I consider the allegation of many that I should not oppose the multitude an open heresy. It can, indeed, be read in sacred utterances that the multitude, as a rule, errs, and that very often one solitary man can put all the rest to flight.[1]

In appointing Saint Peter to be the head and sovereign of all the faithful, Christ assigned to his power certain limits which he was not to overstep. That Christ did not give him a plenitude of power in temporal matters can be proved by authority and reason.[2] But not even in spiritual matters is he endowed with such plenitude of power, because, then, the law of the Gospel, which Saint James, in his canonical letter, chapter 1, calls a "law of perfect liberty," would impose a

[1] *De Imperatorum et Ponticum Potestate,* Proem., 6 Editio: K. C. Brampton, (Oxford: Clarendon Press, 1927).

[2] Ibid., I, 3.

greater servitude than the law of Moses.[3] Saint Peter
did not receive such plenitude of power either in temporal or spiritual matters. Whenever, therefore, the
pope, in case of necessity, meddles in temporal affairs,
he is thrusting his sickle in alien crops, unless he be
entrusted with power to do so by the emperor or by
some other person.[4]

Christ did not come to deprive men of their possessions and rights. Therefore, his vicar, who is smaller
than, he, being not at all his equal in power, has no
rights to deprive others of their possessions and rights.[5]
The papal sovereignty is instituted for the utility and
advantage of its subjects and not for the distinction,
glory, and utility, that is, not for temporal advantage
of the sovereign himself. It really should be regarded
a rule of ministration rather than a rule of domination.[6]

As to how far papal domination can reach, I should
say this : Whatever is possible to a mortal prince and
ruler with reference to the necessities of procuring the
eternal salvation of men and with regard to the rule
and government of the faithful is due to the papal su-
premacy, provided such needs be not extended dispro-
portionately and provided the possessions, rights and
liberties of other people are respected.[7] To explain
generally what I mean by the rights and liberties of
others, of laymen and clergymen, of members of the
religious orders and of the secular clergy, I say that
these are all such things as are not against either good
morals or the teachings of the New Testament. The
freedom of the law of the Gospel praised in the Holy

[3] *De Imp. et Pont. Pot.,* I, 5, and III, 1.
[4] Ibid., II, i. 3.
[5] Ibid., IV, 5.
[6] Ibid., VI, 1.
[7] Ibid., VIII, 1.

Scripture requires that no Christian should be deprived
of such by the pope except in case of guilt or for some
reasonable and manifest cause.[8]

Church regulations which assert that we have to obey
the pope in everything are to be understood with ex-
ceptions.   Otherwise, the papal power would be equal
to the divine power and could, with imperial right, deprive kings and princes and every human being of em-
pires, kingdoms, sovereignties and in general of all
their possessions and take them over and keep them
or assign them to any other person, no matter how con-
temptible the person may be.   Such conduct certainly
would take away and destroy the perfect freedom of
the law of the Gospel.[9]

In the same spirit, scientific assertions, especially
those of the realm of natural philosophy which are not
related to theology, are not to be condemned by anybody in a solemn way nor to be forbidden.   In such
things everybody ought to be free to say freely whatever he pleases.   And, therefore, when a certain archbishop (Robert Kilwardby of Canterbury) condemned
and forbade grammatical, logical, and purely physical
opinions, his sentence should be reputed as one of
temerity.[10]

The community of the faithful has to be subordinated
to a single ruler and supreme judge with regard to all
the causes and cases which may occur.   Otherwise, it
would not be well ordained having either many rulers
or no ruler at all, both of which are to be adjudged
as monstrous.[11]   The pope is the head and supreme

[8] *De Imp. et Pont. Pot.,* IX, 1.
[9] Ibid., XI, 1.
[10] *Dialogus,* I, liber II, c. 22.
[11] *De Imp. et Pont. Pot.,* XII, 1.

judge of all the faithful under Christ. Not so the emperor, who must not concern himself with spiritual matters, not even occasionally.[12]

The church of Avignon tries to rule over all Christians tyrannically, inflicting upon the faithful of Christ serious and enormous injustices. To do this more freely and without any fear, she persecutes tyrannically all those who dare to start an argument about her powers, even though they do it with the best of motives. Thus it comes about that in the universal and other studies, no doctor or master dares even to offer or accept a thesis for debate and determination with reference to the power of the pope. At the same time, such debates about the papal power ought to be pleasing both to the pope and to his subordinates, and welcomed by them, inasmuch as knowledge of the what and how and why with reference to the power of the pope, is necessary for both parties.[13]

The church of Avignon does an especial wrong to the Roman Empire by claiming greater temporal right over it than over other kingdoms. This church does not possess such prerogative over the Roman Empire either by divine or human right.[14] The Roman Empire was earlier than the papacy. Its inceptions did not spring from the pope and, consequently, it cannot be subjected to the pope after the institution of the papacy.[15] A further wrong is done to the Roman Empire by the church of Avignon in the latter's claim that it is her right to admit or approve the person elected to be king or emperor of the Romans. According to this

[12] *De Imp. et Pont. Pot.*, XII, 2.
[13] Ibid., XV, 1.
[14] Ibid., XVII, 2.
[15] Ibid., XIX, 1.

view the elected person cannot rightfully assume his title and office, nor can he begin the administration of the realm or empire without such admission or approbation. The pope, indeed, has no greater right over the empire or over the person of the emperor than over other countries and other kings. But other countries and other kings, at least the majority of them, are not completely subjected to the pope.[16] The pope has no power to dominate the emperor in this way, just as he has no power to dominate other kings in the same manner. Usage cannot warrant such subjection, because usage has no legal virtue at law unless it is reasonable. Such usage, however, introducing this subjugation of the emperor would not be reasonable.[17]

The church of Avignon, further, does injustice not only to the Roman Empire but, as regards ecclesiastical affairs, to all Christians too, in a very material way.[18] They usurp a power which they do not possess, depriving the faithful, clergy and laity, of their possessions, rights and liberties. They impose upon their shoulders unsupportable burdens. They instigate warfare among the Christians, sedition and discord, and foment them after instigation. They impose wicked sentences and unjust procedures, trapping the simple minded. They materially impede the progress of science and coerce the more learned and intelligent to submit their intellect to them in captivity, against reason and against the holy scriptures. Innumerable other injustices and excesses could be adduced, whereby they afflict the Christian people, disturb them, seduce them

[16] *De Imp. et Pont. Pot.*, XX, 1.
[17] Ibid., XX, 2.
[18] Ibid., Cap. XXIV, 1.

and try to force them into servitude against the liberty
of the law of Gospel.

It is my conviction that peace will never be confirmed between the occupants of the apostolic seat and
the rest of the Christians, until the clergy and laity,
settle irrefragably and sanction what powers the pope
possesses by divine right. As long as the multiude of
the faithful is ignorant of this, the stubborn strife
between the pope and people will not cease.[19]

[19] *De Imp. et Pont. Pot.,* XXVI, 1.

APPENDIX*

Words of first imposition

widely	strictly
all words which are not of second intention including syncategorematic signs	categorematic signs which are not of second imposition but which signify either.

examples:
all
nobody
somebody
anybody

	second intentions or first intentions

The signs of first intentions, examples:	The sign of something itself not a sign.

genus
species
universal
particular

examples:
man
animal
Socrates
Plato
whiteness
white
good
true

widely	strictly
signifies intentions and words, i. e.,	signifies intentions only

arbitrarily
instituted
signs

widely	strictly
does not signify intentions or signs whether strictly or widely includes syncategorematic words:	stands for signified signs only

verbs
adverbs
conjunctions
etc.

*Cf. Chap. 11, *Summa tot. log.,* pp. 96-9.

Words of second imposition

widely	strictly
signify words, i. e., arbitrarily instituted signs as long as they are significatory but may signify the intention also. Called:	signify words, i. e., arbitrarily instituted signs only, not intention.

"names of names"
  examples:
    noun
    pronoun
    conjunction
    verb
    case
    number
    mode
    tense

      examples:
        conjugation
        declension
        grammatical figures

WRITINGS OF WILLIAM OF OCKHAM[1]
utilized in the Selections
of the present work.

1) Super quatuor libros sententiarum subtilissimae quaestiones earumdemque decisiones. (Very subtle questions on the four books of the Sentences and their decisions.)

Lyons, 1495

According to Little, Ockham's Commentary on the first book of the Sentences was probably composed when he was a bachelor of divinity at Oxford; it is longer than his commentaries on the other three books together, and it was printed separately at Strassburg in 1483.

2) Quodlibeta septem. (Seven quodlibeta, i. e., miscellaneous treatises.)

Paris, 1487
Strassburg, 1491

At the end of the Strassburg edition we read that this work was published after Ockham's lectures on the Sentences of Peter Lombard given at Oxford. Passages from this book were translated by Prof. Richard McKeon in his Selections from Medieval Philosophers, (Scribner's, New York, 1930) Vol. II., pp. 360-421. With the Strassburg edition was printed Ockham's treatise entitled: "De sacramento altaris et de corpore Christi," translated by T. Bruce Birch, Burlington, Iowa, The Lutheran Literary Board, 1930.

3) Expositio aurea et admodum utilis super artem veterem. (A golden and very useful exposition of the ancient art.)

Bologna, 1496

This book printed, by Benedictus Hectoris, contains Ockham's commentaries to Porphyry's explanations to Aristotle's book on the ten categories and to Aristotle's books on De Interpretatione and the Sophistical Elenchi.

[1] For a full text of Ockham's works the reader is advised to recur to the following book: Andrew G. Little, *The Grey Friars in Oxford,* (Oxford, 1892).

4) Summa totius logicae.   (Sum of All Logic.)

The translation incorporated in the preceding pages was
made from the film-copy of the 1488 Parisian edition in
possession of Harvard Library.

Paris, 1488
Bologna, 1498
Venice, 1508
1522
1591
Oxford, 1675

This mighty logical treatise in three parts may be considered as Ockham's chief work.   On the last fly-leaf of the
Cambridge manuscript (Caius Coll. 464) there can be
found a rude portrait of Ockham.

5) Summulae in libros physicorum.   (Little Summaries to the Books on Physics.)

Bologna, 1494
Venice, 1506
Rome, 1637

This little book, also called Philosophia naturalis, has four
parts and presents Ockham's doctrine on various problems
of natural philosophy.   The University of Nebraska has
a very good copy of the Venetian edition.

6) Centilogium Theologicum.   (Hundred Theological Sayings.)

Lyons, 1495

A very short work containing one hundred theological
propositions critically treated.   It is attached to Ockham's
big Commentary to the *Sentences*.   Little quotes the book
as Centiloquium.

7) Dialogus inter magistrum et discipulum de Impera-torum et Pontificum Potestate.   (A dialogue be-tween master and disciple on the power of the em-perors and popes.)

Lyons, 1495

One of the numerous political treatises of Ockham in three

parts. It was also published in M. Goldast's *Monarchia* II, Frankfurt, 1614 and lately by R. Scholz, *Unbekannte kirchenpolitische Streitschriften aus der Zeit Ludwig des Bayern,* II. Teil, Rome 1914, pp. 392-480.

8) De imperatorum et pontificum potestate. (On the power of the emperors and popes).

Oxford, 1927

A remarkable treatise translated lately by Kenneth C. Brampton, (Oxford, Clarendon Press, 1927). The original manuscript is in the British Museum: Royal 10 A, XV (sec. XIV).

DATE DUE

11-2?